# Under One Roof

# Under One Roof

*The Story of a Christian Community*

**ROGER SAWTELL**

DARTON·LONGMAN+TODD

First published in Great Britain in 2015 by
Darton, Longman and Todd Ltd
1 Spencer Court
140 – 142 Wandsworth High Street
London SW18 4JJ

ISBN 978-0-232-53173-2

A catalogue record for this book is available from the British Library

Phototypeset by Kerrypress Ltd, Luton
Printed and bound by Bell & Bain, Glasgow

# *CONTENTS*

# *Introduction by Jean Vanier*

Let me begin by thanking Roger for this beautiful book. There is not enough written about community and yet it is a reality that concerns every one of us. How can we come together with our differences, with our similarities, with our capacity to be annoying, with our capacity to be kind, with our needs, with our gifts? How can we share a kitchen, a living room, a garden, a table, a laugh or two? How can we grow to forgive each other? What does it take to celebrate together? These are questions that we share, questions that come up again and and again over a lifetime.

Many of us will find that living together is a very frightening prospect. We prefer to have our space, our own apartment, our own projects, our own possessions, our own responsibilities, our own problems, our own successes. And yet Roger's book tells of the incredible gift when we dare to share all of these, when we dare to live in community. The Neighbours differed in age, in way of life, in political opinion, and in manner of worship. They were not particularly brave or daring individuals. They were just a group of ordinary people who, together, lived something quite extraordinary.

This book tells a story of growth, for community is about growth. The Neighbours Community began in little ways, a coffee here, a meal there, a place to stay for a night or two. But over twenty-three years there were many people welcomed under the roof: people who needed a home, people who needed a place to meet, people who simply needed a coffee in the morning. The Community grew as a source of life, deepening in mission and in love.

Growth is not easy. We might say that the way of growth in community is forgiveness. The Neighbours Community was not always a harmonious experience. Indeed community is always messy. There are little frictions, debates and disagreements, failures to find common ground. But each of these is an occasion for growth. When living together, we learn how to approach one another and say, I am sorry. We learn to welcome the other with mercy. We learn when we must speak, and when we must listen. And it is in the day to day moments of discord and reconciliation that we are changed.

Community is a place of forgiveness, but it is also a place of celebration. We celebrate one another because we are happy to be together. We celebrate all that is given in our life together because it is more than we could have asked or imagined. We celebrate our hope for the future, for this adventure continuing. The Neighbours Community closed in 2007, but the fruits of those twenty-three years continue to give life.

To some, Roger's account may seem a light read. There are whimsical details, funny episodes, small dramas, and witty commentary. And yet this book bears an important witness to our world. For in many ways, we live in a world of fear rather than forgiveness, a world of walls rather than open doors, a world of isolation and violence rather than encounter and mediation. We live in a world that in many ways seems to have forgotten the importance of living together. Community life is not a calling reserved for the few. It is a vital necessity for each of us. It is a vital necessity for a world of peace. Because the reality is that we are all *Under One Roof.*

JEAN VANIER
Trosly-Breuil, France
*October 2014*

Jean Vanier is the founder of L'Arche and author of many books, including the classic *Community and Growth.*

# *Preface*

My sad friend, who has atheistic tendencies, said, 'Are you telling me that you are seriously thinking of selling your nice 5-bedroom detached house on Daffodil Close and going to join those religious weirdos living in one of those squalid terraces down by the railway yard?' This is an exaggeration of what we did, of course, but it indicates the misunderstandings and occasional comments we received when Susan and I decided to join our friends Michael and Anne Jones to form a small residential Christian community in 1984. However, the majority of comments were more positive and over a period of forty years discussing, living and writing about communities in this post-Christendom era, it has been a joy to meet so many people on the same journey, some of them inspirational followers of Jesus. We were fortunate to have Rosalind Bellerby and Sister Lucy as advisers and supporters. Others helped, too many to mention all by name, and some have since died.

Susan showed her usual loving forbearance as I grumbled about the writing difficulties and sometimes the words had to be unwillingly wrung out of my head and onto the computer screen. I am grateful for the assistance of former members of The Neighbours Community and for Simon Villette who combed through the drafts and made helpful comments. So did Michael Jackson, now physically disabled (but not mentally or spiritually) by motor neurone disease, unable to hold a book but able to comment on my draft from his computer screen. Daniel Rutland from Servants made a significant contribution to the text and Philip Munch, hermit friend, provided relevant books which were new to me. David Moloney and Helen Porter, together with the team at Darton, Longman and Todd, were wonderfully supportive. The errors, omissions and prejudices are mine alone.

I have focused on small intentional communities 'under one roof' as this is my direct experience and this is a personal story rather than a guide to community living. A friend, who was a regular visitor to The Neighbours, read the draft manuscript and commented that '*you slightly understate the revolutionary nature of what was happening in the formation and development of The Neighbours*'. He added, '*I found myself reflecting that The Neighbours had members with three lives: family, work and community. An enormous internal tension which monastic communities do not have. In many ways it was a miracle of grace that it lasted so long....*'

Grace? The unmerited favour of God towards us. I am told that we all dream every night but it is rare for me to recollect a dream. However, last night, I dreamed that a group of us had entered a large church and were kneeling at the altar rail, waiting for a blessing. But no one came, so we realised that we were in the wrong place and moved to another part of the church, where we received the bread and wine of communion. I take this dream to mean that it is our responsibility to put ourselves in 'the right place' if we are to receive grace. I am 87 now, and if anything I have written is in the right place, I hope it will catch the imagination of younger people travelling the community road.

ROGER SAWTELL
Northampton
*November 2014*

## CHAPTER 1

# A question of definition: What is a community?

*'When I use a word,' Humpty Dumpty said, 'it means just what
I choose it to mean – neither more nor less.'*
*Through the Looking Glass*, Lewis Carroll (1871)

The word 'community' has a number of different meanings. We talk about 'the community' meaning all the people living in a certain area. In a different setting our friend who is an organic farmer writes about '*communities of bacteria and fungi living around crop roots … which help protect our crops from disease*'. This concept would appeal to Jean Vanier, the founder of L'Arche who writes in his seminal work *Community and Growth*:

'*When I use the word "community" I am talking essentially of groupings of people who have left their own milieu to live with others under the same roof and work from a new vision of human beings and their relationships with each other.*'

Communities such as L'Arche might be regarded as the 'bacteria and fungi' which help to protect the wider community from some of the social diseases which beset us, such as isolation, mental illness, lovelessness. Vanier writes with authority because he has lived in L'Arche communities for over half a century. He defines the two essential elements of life in community as a sense of belonging and a common purpose.

The phrase 'intentional communities' has passed into the language, meaning a group which has come together not by happenstance, but by specific intention to live an alternative lifestyle. By living under the same roof the members of such a community are inevitably closer to each other than members of a gathered church congregation in which each person or family lives in their own space and location.

To add to this variety of alternative living styles there is also the concept of a 'commune' in which a group of people share not only their living and eating space but also their income and possessions with a 'common purse'. Also there are 'co-housing' projects in which each household has a separate house, often grouped round a square, with some common facilities such as a meeting room, laundry room or garden. Such groups do not necessarily share the same faith or philosophy, but are closer to one another than 'normal' living in a village or an urban estate or whatever.

The Neighbours Community was not a commune nor a lay monastery nor co-housing, but it was an intentional community under one roof and described itself as a Christian residential 'community of households' within which a 'household' might be a single person, or a couple or a family with children. Each household had its own front door and its own living space. We had a common fund for the shared garden and meeting room but we did not share incomes or all possessions. The essentials were to pray together every morning, share some meals and be aware of each other's strengths and weaknesses. We did not take vows but there was an understanding that members would stay for several years rather than months. Such communities, which can happen in various locations 'on the street', are responses to the Christian gospel.

Out of this welter of words, I have adopted the following definition for the purposes of this book:

A Small Residential Christian Community (SRCC) is a group of people who:

- live under one roof,or closely adjacent roofs on one site.

- pray/worship together regularly, daily or at least weekly.

- eat together regularly, daily or at least weekly.

- have a common task, such as caring for disadvantaged people or running a retreat centre or hospitality or mutual support.

By this definition organisations such as the Iona Community, with a large dispersed membership, or L'Arche with houses all over the world, are not small residential communities, but houses within such organisations (such as the Staff Resident Group on Iona or individual L'Arche houses) do meet the definition. Similarly, a local monastic house within a dispersed religious order such as the Benedictines is a small residential community, as defined. The definition excludes groups which do not live on the site of their common task; for example, some retreat centres and other specifically Christian projects are administered by staff who live in the area and come into work by the day.

With reference to definitions, a significant situation occurred in 1998 when the minimum wage legislation was being debated in Parliament. Most people concerned with fair pay supported this legislation and communities did too but realised that their resident members and volunteers might have to be classified and remunerated as 'hourly-paid employees', an arrangement which would be inappropriate and detrimental to the ethos of the community. Resident members of Christian communities do not necessarily have fixed working times and it may not be easy to distinguish between times when they are 'working' or 'not working'. For example, Chapter VII of the Benedictine Rule refers to *the work of God in the oratory*, and there are numerous further references to prayer in the Rule as '*the work*' of the monastery. It conjures up a crazy picture of monks solemnly 'clocking-in' as they enter chapel for Matins and then 'clocking-out' to make an official record of their working hours.

So a delegation of representatives of intentional communities took up this matter with civil servants and a member of the Sheldon Community writes:

> The meeting at the Department of Trade & Industry turned out to be a waste of time because it was civil servants telling us how to live with the legislation and that, as primary flagship Government legislation, hell would likely freeze over before any concessions were made. Bishops in the Lords didn't want to touch us which was really really disappointing … However, the MP of the Findhorn Community was the first parliamentarian to seriously take up the cause and it was probably that route that got the result. We were told a few weeks before the legislation was passed that some sort of exemption would be provided but it wasn't until 5pm on the day before it came into law that they put the exemption through … For several years we were routinely picked up on the Government's Annual Survey of Hours and Earnings and had to justify our exemption, so it has proved vital for us.

The result of this spirited challenge to bureaucracy was that the Regulations attached to the National Minimum Wage Act 1998 specified that it did not apply to '*a resident member of a community ... if a purpose of the community is to practise or advance a belief of a religious or similar nature ... and all or some of its members live together for that purpose.'* (National Minimum Wage 1998. Regulations. Section 44A. Religious and other communities: Resident workers.)Thus, communities were able to continue to have 'resident workers' who were not subject to the provisions of this Act.

Traditional vowed monastic orders have been exempted from various Parliamentary Acts for many years but these 1998 Regulations to the National Minimum Wage Act had the unexpected side-effect of providing, for the first time, a legal definition of unvowed intentional communities, either religious or secular. As well as the Christian communities under discussion, the term *'or similar nature '* brings in non-religious intentional communities concerned with the environment or other good causes.

*CHAPTER 2*

# Some history of intentional communities

In the early days of Christianity there were no church buildings and 'the church' was more literally 'the people', the believers, meeting and worshipping in each other's houses. Paul the apostle writes *'to our friend and fellow-worker Philemon and the church that meets in your house'* and passages in Acts (2:43-45) indicate that there was more sharing among Christians than we find today. After monasteries began to appear in the third century, gradually a distinction became evident between the monks, who had taken life vows of poverty, chastity and obedience, and lay brothers who were part of the monastic community but did not take vows nor take a full part in the prayer which Benedict declared to be the 'work' of the monks. The lay brothers did much of the manual work to maintain the life of the monastery.

Over the centuries there have always been communities of households, groups of lay Christians, some single, some families, living under one roof and accepting a common discipline. There have been, of course, countless variations of such community lifestyles, some rigorous and some vague and relaxed and many in between. Their detailed history is beyond the scope of this book but a few landmarks of community activity during my lifetime will help to put The Neighbours Community into context.

Most communities are the result of much thought, prayer and discussion, because to move away from the generally accepted living arrangements of the time, possibly to leave the shelter of the family home in order to share money and space with others is a decision of fundamental importance So it is unsurprising that communities of households often have a long gestation period.

For example, the Iona Community grew out of George MacLeod's long association with people of the Govan area of Glasgow during the depression years of the 1930's, but it was not till 1938 that the community coalesced round the restoration of Iona Abbey. The re-building of the monks' living space symbolised the growth of a common life of work and prayer among a very mixed social group of craftsmen and trainee ministers. The young men became builder's mates and the craftsmen were introduced to a pattern of worship which they had not come across even if they had ventured into the churches of suburban Glasgow.

The Bruderhof in Germany came from a very different background. '*A communal movement of families and single men and women who seek to put into action Christ's command to love God and neighbour.*' This concept of a Christian brotherhood was at total variance to Nazi belief in a German super-race and the Gestapo closed the community in 1942 and imprisoned three of the members. Surprisingly, in the middle of the chaos of World War II, the remaining community members managed to travel to England and gradually built up a large residential community at Robertsbridge in Sussex, with its own school and workplace. In 2014 it has grown to about 300 people, half of whom are children. The Bruderhof staunchly uphold the sanctity of Christian marriage and the figures indicate that they do not take a vow of chastity.

After World War II there was a surge in the numbers and variety of residential communities. David Clark, a Methodist Minister and lecturer at Westhill College in Birmingham, began collecting information about Christian groups and communities outside of church congregations. This led to a Community Congress in 1980 in Birmingham to which 250 people came with great enthusiasm to form a coherent movement. This indeed was something new and exciting and David's energy and organising ability led to the formation of NACCAN (National Association of Christian Communities and Networks) with him as Director, and the publication of a Directory of Christian Groups, Communities and Networks.

A Second National Congress took place in 1984, the year that The Neighbours Community started, with similar numbers and similar enthusiasm and the Second Edition of the Directory listed 384 entries. Thereafter there was an annual gathering of NACCAN but no further national Congresses to match these two seminal events. Nine years later, in 1993, the Third Edition of the Directory was more focused on communities rather than non-residential networks and groups and listed 162, of which 106 were inter-denominational and 85 were residential. In 1995 forty people came to a regional NACCAN event at The Neighbours and I became involved with the magazine *Christian Community* and edited it for five years, reporting news from numerous communities and commissioning writing from key figures such as Jean Vanier and Timothy Radcliffe who at that time was Master of the worldwide Dominican Order.

The early 1990s proved to be a high tide of residential communities and by the time the fourth and last edition of the Directory appeared in October 2000, the number of entries had declined to 134. NACCAN disbanded in 2003 due to falling interest and consequent lack of funds. The network *Diggers & Dreamers* continues to publish on their website (www.diggersanddreamers.org.) information about all kinds of community living but there are no more recent figures available for specifically Christian communities. Well-known communities such as Iona, Lee Abbey and Corrymeela continue but a number of other residential communities which flourished in the latter years of the twentieth century have closed and not many new ones are starting at the time of writing (2014). Perhaps it was not surprising that The Neighbours Community, as described hereafter, was unable to find replacements for the Tickle family and for Susan and myself when we decided to move on in 2007.

## CHAPTER 3

# The Neighbours Community 1984-2007

This chapter is an account of The Neighbours Community, drawn from thirteen minute books containing over 3000 minutes over a period of twenty-three and a half years. A Summary and Critique can be found on p.95. Susan and I were the only people to be part of the Community for the whole of its life and the following account is a personal view, part of my life story.

The Neighbours Community was not a commune, neither was it a monastery as we did not take vows nor wear habits. There was little sign of poverty amongst us and even less sign of chastity as, at one stage, the children living in the Community outnumbered the adults. Obedience, whatever that means, was hardly discussed but debate about the right way forward was frequent and sometimes troublesome. Because we had demolished the fences between the five Community houses to make one large back garden, it was possible and customary for members to go from one household to another either through internal doors or via the garden which was common to all. In this way it differed from an ordinary row of terrace houses where it is necessary to go into the street to get from one to the other. It may seem a small difference but this inter-connectedness was a major factor in the life of the community.

Cold callers working their way down Ardington Road were sometimes alarmed to meet the same person responding to the front door bell in each house.

It is rare to have such a detailed week-to-week record of this counter-cultural project and although some of the minutes may seem trivial (e.g. 'Richard reported that he had seen a rat in the cellar'), they were important at the time and contributed to significant changes in our family life. As I get older I find my memory plays tricks and sometimes I recollect what I hoped had happened rather than what actually did happen. As the man said (was it George Bernard Shaw? It's usually him), '*I'm an old man and I've known many troubles, most of which never happened*', so I have been grateful for these minute books as a reliable record. They remain available as an archive and resource and I hope someone may use them in due course to write an independent and objective account.

## The planning years

Soon after we moved from Sheffield to Northampton in 1968 Susan and I were part of a house group of nine people, attached to the parish church of St Peter's, Weston Favell. We called it a 'cell group' and, later, a 'house communion group'. It became an influential part of our lives as we met every other Saturday for ten years, sharing a simple meal, studying the Bible, celebrating Holy Communion and discussing what it means to be Christians in a post-Christendom age.

From time to time the children got drawn into this group, whether they liked it or not, and we went away for a family holiday together every year at February half term, sometimes to Lee Abbey in Devon and sometimes to the Lake District. Often the discussion would revolve round the problems of being the church, the followers of Jesus, in the hedonistic surroundings of the 1970s.

The first entry, in what became Volume 1 of the Community minute books, is an 'aunt sally' piece about the possibility of community living, written in June 1974. It refers to Acts 4:32 and suggests that 'existing terrace houses could be adapted'. We were not thinking of a 'commune' in which everyone lived together but a 'community of households' in which several families might live in separate houses, adjacent to each other, sharing some possessions and adopting some common social concerns. In the meantime, living in separate houses a mile apart, each cell family made a list of what might be shared. It became known as the 'lawnmower list' but also included three bicycles, a dog, a motor caravan, a sewing machine, a folk guitar and two spare beds.

Susan and I were Associates of the Iona Community in Scotland and the next entry is *Columban Houses - Draft Discussion Document* sent to us in 1982 by Ron Ferguson, Leader of the Community. Several models of possible residential communities are described:

> Here's one model: four single people living in a Council house ... two are Protestants, one Roman Catholic, one not sure about anything. They have links with Iona. They have some meals in common, and have daily worship. Here's another model: two houses in one street, one a family, the others single people. All working. They have some meals and worship in common. They are a base for the peace movement in the area. Another model: two houses in nearby streets. Meet for worship, food. Have healing services and specialise in taking 'wounded' people for a spell. Buy food together and share transport.

Ron Ferguson wrote a covering letter (13.12.82) asking us to keep in touch and let him know whatever we decided to do. Although The Neighbours Community did not become specifically linked with the Iona Community, we were much influenced by the Columban House vision and, in due course, adopted a number of the ideas in his discussion paper, several houses in one street, interdenominational, meals together, daily worship, healing services, 'wounded' people.

By 1982, eight years after our initial discussions, I was working at Daily Bread Co-operative and talking and writing about the possibilities of moving towards a more committed and sharing home lifestyle. Susan was working as an Occupational Therapist at St Edmund's Hospital, our children were all away or at university, and we were ready to make a move. The Iona paper gave us a nudge. Susan and I knew that a decision to move from a typical middle-class house in Weston Favell to an uncertain alternative lifestyle would turn our lives upside down and we made the decision with our eyes wide open. There were few precedents for the kind of residential community we had been discussing and we realised there would be all manner of problems to overcome. We reckoned it was 'only worth doing' if we regarded it as a twenty-year project. In the event, we stayed for over twenty-three years.

In 1968, I had got to know Michael Jones because he was planning to turn the family jeweller's business, which he had inherited, to employee-ownership. I was able to assist with preparing the constitution to transform the business into a registered co-operative society under the Industrial & Provident Societies Acts. At the time of writing the business continues to flourish with a turnover of around £5 million and 33 people working in it. Michael has written his life story, *It May be Christian, I think it's Silly*, published in 2009.

Anne Jones had initially worked at the local newspaper and considered a career as a journalist, but she later qualified as a teacher with a degree in English Literature. Michael was a Reader in the Church of England and both of them had been members of the house communion group since its inception.

So in 1982 the four of us began to look for three adjacent terrace houses but realised that finding three for sale at the same time was a very long shot. One day we looked at a house in Ardington Road, in a suburban area of Northampton, which seemed right. It was solidly built and had a long back garden facing west. But we needed three houses, not just one. So Michael knocked at the door of the adjacent house and said, 'Excuse me for asking but I wonder if your house is for sale?'. The young man who answered door said, 'Strange you should ask because my mother died recently and I am about to put this house on the market. Come in and look round'. I knocked on the door on the other side and was confronted by a friendly grey-haired woman. 'Excuse me for asking but I wonder if your house is for sale?' She replied, 'Strange you should ask. My sister lives across the road and I always sleep at her house, not here, so I think I might sell. Come in and have a look round.' This seemed like an answer to our prayers and within a few weeks we had bought all three at a cost of about £20,000 each.

A member of the house communion group, Maurice Walton, was a distinguished architect and he drew up an imaginative plan to make a flexible 'community house' with communicating doors and ten bedrooms. From the road the houses were unchanged but once inside the door it was quite different. The 'front room' of the middle house became our meeting room and, as a symbolic act of sharing property, we knocked down the middle two fences to make a large back garden. Michael and Anne moved into 146 in May 1983, while the builders reconstructed 142 and 144. They were covered in dust for six months but were then able to move into 142 while the builders renovated 146. After a further six months the alterations were completed and we moved in to 146, so that the start date of the community was 29 June 1984. Later we added two further adjacent houses, as will be related, to make five in all.

During the early years we had many discussions about the purpose of the project and members had differing ideas about what we were trying to do. We knew that by joining together we would be capable of caring for disadvantaged people in a manner which could not be done by a single household and it soon became clear that our concern should be for people with mental disorders. Providing supportive accommodation became our corporate task although it was not until 1997 that we adopted a concise statement of purpose:

> The purpose of The Neighbours is to develop a Christian community life which enables us to share and explore our faith and care for others, according to the Gospel.

Thereafter, this statement was printed on all our programmes and remained unchanged throughout the lifetime of the Community.

## The Members

In the same way that the heart of a monastic community is the vowed monks or nuns, the heart of our lay community was the Members:

| | | |
|---|---|---|
| Michael & Anne Jones (142) | June 1984 – May 1994 (10 years) | (with Hannah and Daniel) |
| Susan & Roger Sawtell (146) | June 1984 – December 2007 (23½ years) | (with Mary, Rebecca and Peter) |
| Richard & Jayne Hall (148) | September 1985- September 1990 (5 years) | |

| | | |
|---|---|---|
| Claire Caddick (140) | November 1987- April 1998 (10½ years) | (married Chris 1995. Dominic born 1996) |
| John & Jenny Parkin (148) | March 1991- May 1998 (7 years) | (with Chloe) |
| Deborah Tickle (142) | July 1994 – December 2007 (13½ years) | (with Emily, Claire, Joe. Rowan born 1995) |
| Simon Tickle (142) | July 1994 – July 2004 (10 years) | |
| Richard & Patricia Appleby (140) | April 1998 – December 2007 (9½ years) | (with Matthew, Sarah, Chris and Jonathan) |
| Pam Frier (148) | June 1998 – December 2007 (9½ years) | |
| Stephan Ball (144) | October 2003 – December 2007 (4 years) | |

Over the lifespan of the Community there was a total of 9 'households' comprising the 15 Members listed above. The longest tenure was twenty-three and a half years, and the shortest was 4 years. Including the fifteen Members a total of over 50 people lived in the Community houses at one time or another. This figure does not include friends or relatives coming for a visit but does include people who needed some support, usually on discharge from psychiatric hospital. They were invited to rent room space and join in the life of the

Community, including meals, prayers and social events. Some
stayed a few weeks and some for several years. Some took an
active part in the corporate life, others almost no part.

Quotations from the minute books are shown in *italics*.
(For confidentiality, the names of people with mental health
problems have been changed.)

### Year 1, 1984

The founder members, Michael and Anne and Susan and
I, had been meeting informally for at least a year while the
houses were being modified, sometimes on site with Maurice
Walton, but these meetings were not recorded. After we moved
in we held the first minuted meeting of the community on 28
September 1984. Thereafter, in various handwritings, some
more legible than others, the minute books record the total life
of the community.

### Year 2, 1985

In that vital first year we did not appear to have regular daily
prayers and this was seen to be rather shocking to some of
our clerical friends. We rectified it before long and instituted
morning prayers at 7.30 a.m. Everyone living in the houses
was invited as a matter of course; some came every day, some
not at all. It was totally interdenominational and at one time
or another, we had Anglicans, Roman Catholics, Quakers, and
Methodists. Although the liturgies used varied extensively, I do
not recollect many theological or church order problems with
such ecumenical occasions and wondered if Christian unity
would eventually come 'from the edges', the radical fringe,
rather than from the central church bodies.

Alongside major decisions there are dozens of minutes
of the small practical details of adjacent living including
vital comments such as *pudding cooked by Edith and games
will be played and Michael will join in!*, a stern rebuke to any
community member who might choose to read a book rather

than take part in jolly games. Susan *requested indoor fireworks* at our first Christmas dinner in the community room (which later we called The Neighbours Room). Anne's father, Ernie Croft, stood stolidly in front of the open fire telling stories of his eventful life and desisted only when his trousers were in imminent danger of bursting into flames.

As a symbol of a sharing which was new to all of us, for grace before meals, we held hands with *thumbs to the right*, one hand giving and the other hand receiving. We ended evening meetings by saying Compline together, a historic part of Benedictine liturgy which begins with the rather disturbing advice, '*Your adversary the devil prowls around like a roaring lion seeking someone to devour. Resist him, firm in your faith.*' (1 Peter 5) The nearest we had to a roaring lion was the elderly community cat which we thought was slightly mad.

Michael was anxious to regularise the position of Edith Crowe who had worked for his mother for many years and then come to live with them in Booth Lane. Michael and Anne had undertaken to give her a lifetime home and when they moved into 142 we all accepted that she should live independently in the flat on the upper floor of 144 for as long as she wished to do so.

Edith was not on the prayer or supper rotas but played an important part in the community by providing an informal daily 'coffee morning' in her flat for anyone who was at home during the day. This was often an unthreatening lifeline for fragile residents. Her tenancy arrangement was regularised by letters with Becke Phipps, Solicitors. A note about community supper in 1992 reads *Edith's steam pudding as usual.* She must have made hundreds, if not thousands, of steam puddings and in her unobtrusive manner she had been a wonderful help to the Jones family for almost fifty years. Michael and Anne generously acknowledged this by giving her security and a continuing role in her old age. In due course, Edith moved on with them in 1994 when they left The Neighbours and continued to live in their house in Weston Favell and thereafter at St John's Home until she died in 1999 aged 86.

Meetings of The Neighbours in the 1980's were sometimes about theological concepts such as the meaning of '*your Kingdom come*' but much more time was taken up with discussions about gardening or washing. For example, in January 1985 we reflected on Anne's *intensive use of the (shared) washing machine*. She defended her *thirteen washes per week at an average of one hour per wash*. We had, of course, inherited the culture of the time which in Ardington Road decreed a tidy garden and no washing to be hung out on Sundays which seemed a bit strange as not many went to church on Sundays and full-time workers often needed to do their washing at the weekend rather than on the traditional Monday washday. We also had student children coming home for the weekend with piles of washing. Edith was a key figure in the clothes washing and drying routines and hardly a day went by without her asking Susan whether or not it was going to rain. A minute reports that she *asked about drying in the utility room on Sundays* and the members appeared solemnly to have decided that there was no theological objection to this procedure. We accepted the Sunday ban on the garden washing line, *except in emergencies*, but the nature of such emergencies was not spelt out. Pants were acceptable on weekdays but should not be displayed on Sundays. The domestic details of a counter-cultural semi-communal lifestyle were constant features of discussion and if we spent too much time on 'the things that are eternal' we were soon brought down to earth.

When we added 148 Ardington Road to the community houses we dismantled another fence so that we had four narrow gardens knocked into one. Later, we added the garden belonging to 140 to make a total of five. The frontage of the houses on the road was unchanged and visitors entering any of the houses were surprised to go out of the back doors into this open space with lawns and some large trees. Plans for the garden were often on the agenda.

We moved the pond, considered a second pond with carp, planted trees some of which grew so large that they had to topped or felled during the twenty year span. Susan's aunt gave us a seedling for a Judas tree which withstood the ravages caused by the children's football and, with tender care, grew into a bush two metres high.

Michael, a keen gardener, would come back from work and go straight out into the garden with his hoe to wind down He was proud of the hydrangeas in the front, especially a white one, which was unusual and admired by passers-by. Later, in the 1990s, John Parkin grew vegetables and there is a photo of him beaming over a cornucopia of vegetables in a wheelbarrow. Some, like me, did no planting but were organised into working parties for rougher work.

Later on we had family wedding receptions, parties, fund-raising barbecues for the soup kitchen and Caribbean evenings which caused complaints from some of the more respectable neighbours along the road about noisy bands playing late into the night. We responded by inviting them to the next occasion but it caused some friction. None of these events would have been practicable in a single suburban garden.

Before a local election in April we pondered on whether we should put up window posters in the Neighbours Room as *two families vote differently*, indicating that political discussion was on the agenda. Notwithstanding our smouldering agreement to adopt a community neutral stance, Mrs Thatcher remained in power until 1992. Later, we agreed that any household should be free to put posters in their own windows but not in the community room unless the weekly meeting agreed, because this was seen to be a community decision. For example, a Holy Week poster was agreed but not any party political ones. We held the Christian faith in common but did not necessarily agree about how to put it in practice in political terms.

A surprising minute in December 1985 agreed that I should make an offer of £6,150, on behalf of the Community, to buy a field at Molesworth, near Peterborough, where American Cruise missiles with nuclear warheads were said to be sited. The field, where ponies were grazing, inexplicably belonged to the Diocese of Peterborough which was thought to be considering selling it to the Ministry of Defence (MoD) as the area was needed for an entrance to the missile site.

The Neighbours Community had no need of a field 30 miles away and we did not have the money in hand but there was a public debate about nuclear warfare at that time and we considered it to be a political concern we should address. The Neighbours' lobby soon segued into a wider Christian group which became actively engaged with objections to the existence of the Molesworth base. Several of us took part in demonstrations round the perimeter fence and we have a photo of a policeman helping us climb out of a very muddy ditch. None of us was arrested, which was rather a disappointment.

We soon raised promises for the money in case our bid for the field was accepted but, after some controversial exchanges, the Diocese decided not to sell this field, probably for fear of the adverse publicity. The MoD were forced to move their proposed entrance to a point further along the perimeter and at the time of writing, the field remains outside the perimeter fence and ponies are still grazing on it.

Christian CND organised the building of a small chapel near the site, to be a place of witness for peace rather than nuclear war but on 6 April 1986, a few months after it had been built, the MoD demolished it. Thereafter, a Peace Garden was established beside the entrance to the base with a descriptive notice board. Our group saw this strange campaign about the field to be an important Christian witness for peace and I put together a scrapbook of press cuttings, photos and correspondence to stand as a record. (*Molesworth – February 1985 to April 1986.*)

Back in Ardington Road, our neighbour on the north side looked at us with disfavour and muttered about parking problems, but on the south side was Dorothy Seamark, a wonderful elderly Baptist. She told us she had often prayed that some kind of Christian initiative would happen in her house but now she was old and planned to move into Bethany Homestead, a Baptist residential home. 'Would you like to add my house to your community?', she said, so we looked for someone else to join the project and found Richard Hall who had come to work at Daily Bread Co-operative and was engaged to Jayne. They came to supper with us. They had looked at some grotty houses within their price bracket as potential newly-weds and welcomed the possibility of joining The Neighbours. The Joneses and ourselves had sold our larger houses in Weston Favell and had money in hand after buying the Ardington Road houses so we were able to make a loan to enable them to buy 148 at a favourable price from Dorothy Seamark, who was glad to be able to help them join a Christian community.

A small sign outside the house named it *Sheppards Peace*. Dorothy's late husband, Stanley, had been a pacifist and active peace worker with Dick Sheppard, charismatic vicar of St Martin's-in-the Fields in Trafalgar Square during the 1920s. There was a rumour that Gandhi had stayed with the Seamarks during his visit to England but this was discounted. Richard asked that we continue to call the house *Sheppards Peace* which chimed with his own views and we agreed because it would remind us of Dorothy who had been such an unexpected but wonderful neighbour and supporter of our tentative project. The Seamarks had not only been in touch with Dick Sheppard but also with Vera Brittain, another well-known pacifist and author of *Testament of Youth*, a classic and poignant autobiography of World War 1 and the 1920s. The sign has been refurbished and is now outside the house of one of Dorothy's relatives in Northampton.

Richard and Jayne were married in their home town of Pontefract and moved into 148 in September 1985. Jayne decided to train as a librarian but had some difficulty in getting a place on her chosen training course in London. She phoned every week to the course administrator to ask if there was a vacancy and eventually she was successful. We called this determination and refusal to take no for an answer 'the Jayne Hall factor' and encouraged our children to be similarly persistent. Richard and Jayne were members of the community for five years until they moved to Birmingham in 1990 for Richard to go to Queen's College to train as a Methodist minister.

Right from the start we made the front room of 144 into a shared community room to be used as a neighbourhood resource as well as by ourselves for meetings. Various groups began to use it, including the local parish church, Christ Church Stewardship Committee, and *Brother Hubert's healing ministry*, led by a charismatic Afro-Caribbean. This was an early indication of the ecumenical stance of the community as we tried to welcome Christians of *all denominations and none*.

The Order of St Luke held their weekly prayer meeting for healing at 144 for about fifteen years, under the guidance of Ken Thomason, a saintly retired Baptist minister. We called them 'the lukies' and made good friends. When Ken died, aged 93. it transpired that he owned just one pair of shoes and I believe this should be counted to him for righteousness. On hearing about the shoes at Ken's funeral, I returned home and counted fifteen pairs in my cupboard.

Other groups meeting in this room over the years, included a yoga class, a U3A philosophy group, a Julian Group, and Daily Bread Prayer Group. It was a wide selection of Christian-based and local community groups needing a smaller and more comfortable meeting place than the church hall or similar. We considered that this was a useful facility, bought some new chairs and spruced-up the downstairs loo and tea-making equipment in the adjacent utility room where, also, Anne and Susan ran the washing machine, which they considered sometimes made just as tuneful a sound as the lukies' hymn singing.

Spending time with people recently released from psychiatric hospitals we learned that isolation and loneliness was often a problem, as they struggled to re-integrate with the wider world, very different from the relatively closed world of the hospital ward. Sometimes the most depressing time of the week for people living alone is Sunday afternoon when 'nothing ever happens'. In July 1985 Michael proposed we should have an 'open tea' every other Sunday in the Neighbours room. This soon became popular as a mixed gathering, including some of the Ardington Road neighbours, some Community members as well as lonely people and some with mental health problems and low self-esteem. We had to limit the numbers to *three per household*. Sunday Tea became a firm part of the Community ministry and continued for many years.

When the reconstruction of 142/144/146 was completed, an official from the local authority came to re-assess the rates for the three houses which were now inter-connected on the ground floor and the first floor. I showed her round and tried to explain the inter-connections but I could see she was troubled because it was not something she had encountered before. She stood in the garden, where there were now no fences, with her clipboard and gazed at the backs of the houses, deep in thought. Eventually she said she could not identify each separate property any longer and proposed that she assess the rates as if it were one house instead of three. I agreed without hesitation because I knew that the assessment for one large house with nine bedrooms was substantially less than the sum of three houses each with three bedrooms. Synergy infers that the whole is more than the sum of the parts but in this case, the whole is less than the sum of the parts. (There does not appear to be an antonym for synergy.) This decision by the rating officer saved us thousands of pounds over the life of the community.

Composite rating depended, of course, on mutual trust between the constituent households but we had no difficulty in apportioning the total bill between us. There were a number of similar expenses to be distributed such as heating, decorating, and the number of bedrooms in use by each household. This latter varied quite often as siblings came and went as well as people recovering from mental disorders. If the houses had been communally owned all these could have been dealt with by having one corporate account but we did not go down that road, for better or for worse, because we were trying to make it possible for families to join the community without abandoning house ownership.

These considerations led to several Agreements made between members of the community over the years. The first was signed on 21 May 1985 by three households, Jones, Sawtell, Hall. The key clause was that, in the event of a household leaving the community, their house should be *valued by at least two and preferably three estate agents of good reputation (if such can be found)* and a valuation price agreed by all the signatories. The house would then be offered to potential new members at the valuation price. This, of course, is not the same as selling the house on the open market and might lead to difficulties if no buyer came forward straight away, particularly if the housing market was fluid, as it certainly was during the years in question. In a falling market, the arrangement would be to the material advantage of the seller but as the market was usually rising, and sometimes quite sharply, the buyer would have the advantage.

During the 1980s there was a lot of interest in residential Christian communities of various kinds and a national organisation sprang up, the National Association of Christian Communities and Networks (NACCAN). We became early members and Susan went to a weekend conference at Spode House on *Setting Up a Christian Community House*. She reported that, even at that early stage in the development of The Neighbours, she *had not learnt much that we had not already experienced.* Most of the participants were religious orders struggling with fewer vowed monks or nuns and unwieldy inflexible properties.

### Year 3, 1986

The members at the beginning of the year were Michael, Anne, Roger, Susan, Richard, Jayne.

'*Our life and our death is with our neighbour. If we win our brother, we win God. If we cause our brother to stumble, we have sinned against Christ.* '(Anthony the Great, circa AD 300, quoted in *Life of Anthony*' by Athanasius)

On 6 January 1986 we agreed to call ourselves The Neighbours, having had no formal name until then. The name was then set in stone because we commissioned some terracotta plaques from a local potter and fixed one beside each of the five doors on Ardington Road. I still have two of these beautiful plaques, here in our flat. Later, we added the word Community to distinguish our project from a popular TV soap opera called *Neighbours* (which is still running today) and which caused some confusion. Visitors asked 'Are you on TV every night?'

The adoption of this name was partly due to what Michael termed a 'long-awaited' philosophical paper from me about Jack Bellerby. In the early 1930s Jack was Professor of Economics at Liverpool University, a young enthusiastic writer on economics and social theory with a growing reputation in academic circles. Between 1931 and 1933, a group of his friends decided to call themselves The Neighbours and Jack wrote, during the great depression:

> The Neighbours is a society with one rule: to keep personal expenditure within the 'average wage' limits of 60 shillings(£3) per week for a single person, 80 shillings (£4)for a married couple one of whom works in the home, and 10 shillings (50 p) extra for each dependent child. Anyone who sends to the Group Committee an account

of his expenditure showing sincerity in the attempt to live within these limits becomes automatically a member.

Some live on much less, the aim being to save in order to give. Surplus income is either spent by members independently on social aims which concern them, or pooled for works acknowledged by the Society to be creative: that is, works which create the values of truth, beauty and love.

Several have joined The Neighbours because they believe it is a step towards Christian living; others because they think it is a necessary gesture in these acquisitive days; others because they seek happiness through service; others because they believe in simplicity of living; others because they wish for company in giving to their limit; others because they feel that economic and social equality is the necessary basis for a further advance of the human spirit.

During the 1930s The Neighbours met regularly to exchange experience, report on their spending patterns and to support one another. Jack hoped that this group would become a residential community as a Gospel witness of solidarity with the poor (Matthew 19:21) but this did not happen. However, Jack himself lived out his vision by resigning his professorship and moving to a small cottage in Cornwall where he wrote and walked and contemplated, managing to spend not more than the average wage of the day.

Jack uses the term 'average wage' of £3 per week for a single person in 1931 and the context indicates that he means the wage of a typical manual worker. It is interesting to note that the UK average gross weekly earnings in April 2012 was £506 (www.gov.uk) and the National Minimum Wage which for age 21 and over is £6.31 per hour (www.gov.uk) in October 2013,

which equates to £236 per week. These huge increases are not
only due to inflation but also represents the vast change in the
material standard of living during the eighty years since Jack
was writing. Perhaps the better comparison with Jack's £3 is
the so-called 'living wage', defined as the sum needed to live
a normal life without undue hardship. In November 2012, the
*Guardian Weekly* (2.11.12) estimated this to be £7.20 per hour,
or £270 per week. Jack would have had no car, no TV or phone
and no NHS to support him in his remote Cornish cottage but
he was not defeated by the material problems of living on £3
per week. However, he could not afford to travel or buy books
and he abandoned the experiment after two years because this
social and cultural diminishment affected the 'contribution'
to society which was such a primary concern for him. He
returned to academic life at the Oxford Institute for Research
in Agricultural Economics. (For further information about Jack
Bellerby, see Appendix A.)

I had met Jack and his wife Rosalind in 1970 through my
work with employee-owned co-operative businesses and we
became close friends. By then he had retired, living in Oxford,
and I came to regard him as mentor and adviser. Susan reckons
that Jack and Rosalind informally 'adopted' me as the son they
never had. After Jack died in 1977, aged 80, Rosalind remained
a vigorous and generous supporter of the Community which
she saw as an outworking of his philosophy. She also donated to
Daily Bread Co-operative a beautiful tapestry which hangs in
their meeting room and, as will be related, Rosalind provided
the initial funding of The Neighbours Mental Health Trust in
1987. The re-born Neighbours in the 1980s did not attempt
nor aspire to live on minimum wages but, like Jack Bellerby, we
accepted a concern to 'live simply' and not get caught up in the
contemporary race to add to the stock of material goods. For
example the cars owned by community members were mostly
rather elderly and infirm. When a tree fell on to Claire's beloved
but somewhat rusty yellow Renault 4, her insurance company

refused her request to have it repaired but sent it straight to the scrapheap.

On 24 April 1986 an *Agreement concerning 142/144/146 Ardington Road* was signed by the four original community members, Michael, Anne. Roger, Susan, who owned these three houses. The introduction reads:

> As a group of Christians sharing the occupation and ownership of several adjacent houses, we seek God's will and believe it is revealed to us through prayer, discussion and reading the Bible, sometimes suddenly and sometimes slowly and gradually. In this sense the sharing project is an act of faith and therefore most decisions should not be taken in advance but only when they become topical. However, there are some matters which need to be agreed in advance … The procedure by which members may leave the project is one such matter.

The agreement then set out the details of how and when the three houses might be sold if one or both the owning families were to leave. This particular agreement never needed to be used but similar arrangements made with subsequent members were put into effect on four occasions. In 1991 the Halls sold 148 to the Parkins; in 1994 the Joneses sold 142 to the Tickles; Claire Caddick sold 140 to the Tickles for the Applebys in 1998; also in 1998 the Parkins sold 148 to Pam Frier. Two of these sales went through to the satisfaction of all parties, and some significant savings of estate agents fees, around £2,000 for a sale at £100.000, but the other two were not quite so satisfactory. In all four cases, the couple moving on was buying elsewhere, and in two cases the sellers considered they would have got a better price on the open market which was important because they were buying on the open market. At one stage, the legal standing of the agreement was queried but in the event, all parties kept to the agreement they had signed.

These agreements, for all their weaknesses, succeeded in their purpose of maintaining the continuity of the Community and its stated purpose for twenty-three years, but they were controversial and complicated. A better model is needed if lay unvowed residential communities are to flourish. We had examined the possibility of putting the ownership of all the houses into a housing co-operative but this was rejected for fear that leavers would not be able to re-enter the housing market on level terms.

Brian Wilkinson, a Methodist minister from Johannesburg stayed with us for a month in 1986 and we discussed whether or not we should charge him a bed and breakfast rate but *this was met with general disapproval*. Brian wrote an enthusiastic report on his visit but the manuscript has been lost. During his stay with us, he worked as a volunteer at Daily Bread Co-operative, as did a number of visitors. In May 1988 he wrote to say he had been awarded a master's degree (Master of Theology) on the strength of his thesis about Daily Bread. It was Brian who said, *Daily Bread Co-operative is the only supermarket where you may get hugged by the person on the till.*

During 1986 we discussed how we might accept more people needing supportive accommodation and agreed that an additional house, either adjacent or nearby, was the best way forward. It would be a household of people learning to live together in the wider community but needing some help from us, the Community. The former headmaster's house of Northampton School for Boys, just along the road from us was for sale and we viewed it but decided it was too large and it was also inhabited by rats.

These rats found their way along Ardington Road and we heard scurrying footsteps at night in the roof space. Peter, who was studying electronics at Reading University, constructed a complicated rat-trap mechanism of springs, weights and wires, but it failed to lure any rats. We reckoned they were usually one step ahead of us in technology. Then we discovered a nest of them in the cellar of 146 and accepted that they were a threat to health as well as a scare to most people. Reluctantly and squeamishly, I drowned the babies in a bucket and was amazed at the strength of their struggle to survive and realised that this determination was the reason for the survival of rats all over the world, despite great efforts to exterminate them. A few days later I was called to the kitchen of 142, where a large adult rat had been sighted. I threatened it with a rolling pin but it refused to come out from its safe haven, crouching behind the cooker. We sent for the house cat, Sammy, and he and the rat glared at one another. Then Sammy turned tail and fled, leaving the rat in occupation, grinning from ear to ear. (For more information about Sammy, see *In Memoriam*, Appendix C.) Eventually we caught the rat in a monster spring trap. I did not enjoy this process, but we had no further visitations and were glad when builders started to renovate Old School House, as we reckoned the rats had been happily living there in community for years while the house was empty. The rats taught us the need for courage and determination if we wanted to develop a counter-cultural lifestyle.

We had an inspirational relationship with Dorothy Seamark, our initial neighbour on the south side, but a rather more confrontational one with our northern neighbours. There were rumblings about car parking and a tedious year-long debate about the party fence in the back garden. One of the Neighbours' children had allegedly been observed *pissing on the fence* and hardly a month went by without some new complaint about 'those religious people next door'. It was also being said that house values would be affected because of 'mad' people living at 142/144/146. We resisted these views and held that there was no emotional difference in the needs of someone who has broken a leg and those with mental illness. Both need help but the prevailing view was that mental illness was 'a disgrace' and not to be discussed. The NHS spent comparatively little on alleviating it. We said that 'mad' was an unacceptable word for clinical depression or schizophrenia and persevered with our plans.

Then, unexpectedly, the next door house, 140 Ardington Road, came on the market and we decided to buy it, if possible, because it was a chance not to be missed. We knew it would soon sell as, despite our neighbours' dire prognostications about housing blight caused by us, Ardington Road continued to be an attractive area with trees on the pavement and good schools nearby. Our problem was that we did not have the money. However, our good friend Rosalind Bellerby from Oxford, wanting to support her late husband's concerns, offered us an interest-free loan of £36,000. So we bought 140 and then started negotiations with a housing trust, Orbit Housing, to buy it from us for the social purpose of supportive accommodation. These plans eventually came to nothing so we looked for someone to buy the house and join the community.

### Year 4, 1987

The members at the beginning of the year were Michael, Anne, Roger, Susan, Richard, Jayne.

When we were living in Sheffield, Susan and I had come across the Taizé Community in France because Leslie Hunter, Bishop of Sheffield, invited some of the Taizé Brothers to visit Whirlow Grange, the diocesan conference centre. Brother Roger came with several others and the experience of sitting in a circle on the floor of the Whirlow chapel with them, singing the emerging Taizé chants, which later became well known the world over, has remained with me for over half a century.

Frère Jan, an experienced psychologist from The Netherlands, stayed in Sheffield for a year, working as a porter at the Children's Hospital where Susan had also worked as an occupational therapist before our marriage. This was the Taizé pattern of ministry which the Brothers adopted wherever they were in the world, to work at the very bottom of the employment situation and be a quiet Christian presence of service.

We continued to visit Taizé and on one occasion met Claire Caddick who was a probation officer working in Wellingborough. She was interested in joining the Community and buying 140 but, in the space of our temporary ownership the market price had increased to £42,000. Claire was able to negotiate a mortgage for £28,000 and between us we lent her the balance so that she could buy the house and move into it in November 1987, thus becoming the seventh member of the community. This enabled us to repay Rosalind's loan by the agreed date and to offer her the balance of £4,200, but she generously chose to donate the whole of this surplus to the Trust (see p.37). We appreciated this and in 1987 we invited her to be an Honorary Member, one of only two such appointments during the lifespan of the Community. She accepted (see Appendix B) and bequeathed to me a monumental minute book about Jack's activities in the 1930s. We used this as our Minute Book for three years, 1987-89, until it was full. In 1989 Rosalind moved into a nursing home in Oxford and died on 13 January 1992. She was a wonderful friend to the Community, also to Daily Bread Co-operative, and to Susan and myself.

In due course we made a formal Agreement with Claire similar to the one with Richard and Jayne. She took advice from a solicitor who said it seemed to be a 'peculiar arrangement' but not unfavourable to her. This served its purpose of keeping the five houses together but, ten years later, when Claire moved on in April 1998, it caused some difficulty. In retrospect, any such counter-cultural agreements at a time when house prices were rapidly increasing was bound to cause problems and none of us was satisfied that we had found a solution which could be replicated by other people in other places.

We welcomed Claire and this fifth house, but decided that this was enough and we would not disturb the neighbourhood by extending further along the road. We knocked down another fence and this serial fence demolition became a kind of broad symbol of a sharing community, as compared to narrow individual back gardens.

1987 was a year of change for us because Susan, aged 55, decided to retire from her Occupational Therapy work at St. Crispin's Hospital in June and, likewise, I retired from full-time work at Daily Bread Co-operative, aged 60. So we had more time and energy for the emerging community, helping to consolidate the five houses and a stable group of seven members.

Claire's experience as a probation officer helped us to clarify the Community policy regarding people recovering from mental illness. During the 1970s Michael Jones was chairman of the local branch of the mental health charity, MIND, and we became aware of the need for supportive accommodation for people who had been in one or other of the two psychiatric hospitals in the town, St. Crispin's NHS and St. Andrew's, an independent charitable trust, but admitting NHS patients into specialist units such as head injuries and eating disorders.

We decided that our common task at The Neighbours would be to offer accommodation to people discharged from these hospitals, some of whom had nowhere to live because they had been abandoned by their families or because they wanted to make a new start. In due course this concern came to the notice of local residents, some of whom were alarmed that we were bringing 'mad people' into the neighbourhood. 'It will have a disastrous effect on our house prices', they said, but this did not turn out to be the case. Ardington Road, continued to be a 'desirable area' in the books of estate agents who continued to take their fees. Houses like the ones we bought for around £20,000 in 1983 were selling for more than £200,000 in 2014.

Claire's Catholic faith did not prevent her from approving the moves that the Church of England was making regarding women priests and, together with Susan, welcomed the eventual outcome in 1992. We went to the first service at which women were ordained at Peterborough Cathedral where our friend Valerie Barford was top of the alphabetical list of ordinands and therefore became the very first woman to be ordained in the Diocese of Peterborough. There was much rejoicing. Susan had become increasingly impatient with the Anglican patronising attitude towards women and this was one of the factors which led her to move over to the Religious Society of Friends (Quakers) at about this time. The Quakers had accepted gender equality more than a hundred years ago and had long since appointed men and women to their multifarious committees, Elders and Overseers, without any gender bias. Susan found this a breath of fresh air and was also happy with the Quaker style of worship, corporate silence and individual ministry.

During the period 1987-89 there are more than twenty Minutes about house prayers and liturgy and it was at this time that we instituted daily morning prayers which remained a significant part of the life of the community for twenty years.

In 1987 we met Patrick who was about to be discharged from psychiatric hospital and needed somewhere to live because his father was not willing to have him at home. He had been struggling with schizophrenia for a long time and was now working as a warehouse person. His father said 'Why doesn't he get a proper job?' and did not appear to recognise his illness. We invited Patrick to come and live at The Neighbours and he stayed for over six years and is proud of the fact that he is the only person who has lived in each of the five houses. It would have been difficult, almost impossible, for a conventional family to have given a home to Patrick at that stage, but we were able to ask him to move from one house to another, and we all survived. There is no magic cure for his distressing condition and he still suffers from occasional delusional episodes but he has held down a job for over fifteen years, and is now (2014) able to live independently in his own flat, with some help on hand when needed.

During 1985 we had begun to discuss the possibilities of setting up a charitable trust in connection with our involvement with people recovering from mental disorders. This would give the project some legitimacy and, as the accounts of all registered charities must be filed with the Charity Commission, might enable us to attract donations from a wider constituency. We sent our draft trust deed to the Charity Commission in July, noting that *it is known to act with ponderous lack of speed* and they came right up to expectations by sitting on it for months and then, when nudged by us, recommending some minor alterations. The Neighbours Mental Health Trust Deed, Registered Charity No. 296869 was eventually signed on 8 May 1987 by the six current community members, so the setting-up process had taken about two years. The objects are:

> 'To promote the material, mental and spiritual health of people suffering ….. from mental illness or mental disorder and to facilitate the rehabilitation of such people into the social and general life of the community.'

Thereafter, people staying in the houses paid their rent into the Trust and money from groups using the Neighbours Room was also channelled into it, together with the £4,200 donated by Rosalind Bellerby in November 1987. For twenty years, income and expenditure relating to the people living with us was allocated to the Trust which therefore became an integral part of the Community. Since then the Trust has passed through several different phases.

### Year 5, 1988
The members at the beginning of the year were Anne, Michael, Susan, Roger, Jayne, Richard, Claire. Edith was living in the 144 flat and Patrick at 146.

We were firmly opposed to any suggestion of becoming a Sunday congregation and, throughout the whole span of the venture Members were active in their various denominational churches: Church of England, Roman Catholic, Quaker, Methodist. Our liturgy was always specifically ecumenical and inclusive and as the Community became better known we began to receive visitors from overseas, interested in different ways of being the church, defined as Christians gathered together in one place. We had 'banded together' in 1984 and now people wanted to come and have a look at what we were doing.

Susan and I had visited the Taizé Community in France several times and in August 1988 we invited to stay with us at the Community two young women from Shillong, a remote area of north east India. They had been staying for some months at Taizé and were accompanied to Northampton by Jenny and John Parkin, whom we had met at a monthly interdenominational prayer in the style of Taizé which we helped to organise at Northampton Cathedral. Christians were in a minority in Shillong and life there for Virginia and Susan was not easy but they were unfailingly cheerful and a joy to have staying with us. They visited the Parkins at their home in Towcester where Jenny tried to teach them morris dancing. We kept in touch with Virginia and Susan for some years after they returned to India and in 1991, Lyn and Geoff Reeves, friends of The Neighbours, travelled to Shillong to make a return visit. Also in 1991, as will be related, Jenny and John Parkin came to live at The Neighbours.

Bevin Fitzimons came from New Zealand stayed with us in November 1988 and also worked at Daily Bread. He wrote on his return, *I have been particularly helped by your practical Christianity and the anchor that it has in your daily worship. My own worship life has blossomed as a direct result* ….

Such visitors were an encouragement to us as we sometimes felt a little despondent about our witness. Michael Jones *considered we had made little impact in our chosen area of rehabilitation from mental illness.*

The garden was often on the agenda and Michael as the 'lead member' was developing it to be a huge asset which gave pleasure to many residents and visitors. As well as planting shrubs and trees, he made it child-friendly with a large climbing frame and 'soapy slides'. From time to time children fell into the pond. He called for working parties but the response was mixed and in May, when everything was burgeoning, it is recorded that he felt *grumpy* about lack of support. *Neighbours were suitably contrite.* Thereafter Jayne and, in due course Nina, watered the roses and Patrick undertook to mow the lawn when Michael was away. This pleased him and he *invited members to look at the strong, happy and dramatic heliborus by the 140 fence.*

The houses were good for family occasions and as early as 1985 Rachel Jones had had her wedding reception in the garden. Another joy in 1988 was the wedding of our daughter, Ruth, to Nigel Mason at St Peter's Weston Favell, which had been our parish church before we moved to The Neighbours. Our friend, Michael Adie, Bishop of Guildford, married them. Ruth, an experienced hill-walker, insisted that she and her bridesmaids in their wedding finery should *walk* the one mile across the park from The Neighbours to the church. We put up a marquee in the garden for the reception, easily accommodating a hundred people. A year later their daughter, Helen, was baptised by Valerie Barford at St Peter's and we had another party in the garden. Some years later, Rowan Tickle arrived, the first person to be born into the Community, and 25 people came to his baptism celebration in the garden.

### Year 6, 1989
The members at the beginning of the year were Michael, Anne, Roger, Susan, Richard, Jayne, Claire. Edith was living at 144 and Patrick at 148.

We began to discuss the size of the Community. Richard commented that the Thursday meal was becoming *a bit of a problem ... sometimes as many as fifteen people. Perhaps we should modify how we do it.* We were at the limit of the number we could get round the supper table and considered that we should not grow the Community any larger because eating together was a top priority. Over twenty people would be present for Christmas dinner 1989.

We also found that a fortnightly meeting was *insufficient* to get the business done and we should have an intervening weekly discussion time. I had visited some other Christian residential communities and found, to my dismay, that some of their well-respected leaders *had feet of clay*. Sometimes our feet also seemed mired in clay and from time to time tempers frayed. Due to a comparatively trivial double-booking incident, the minute book reports, *Roger was annoyed and felt that we were in breach of hospitality. Michael apologised.* Some members must have considered me overbearing and self-righteous but it seems they were sufficiently forgiving not to record it in the minutes. Despite these emotional setbacks, I do not recollect that Susan or me ever doubted that we had set our feet on a long-distance path, clay or no clay, and were not likely to turn back.

Claire was much involved with disadvantaged people, both in her work and at 140 but our weekly meetings, perhaps unduly influenced by Michael and myself, tended to be dominated by what we saw as practicalities. She nudged us to *talk about something other than business* and this led us in due course to have alternate 'Martha ' and 'Mary' meetings to find a balance.

It is interesting to note that the Quakers had similar dilemmas. Historically, their attention to the 'business' of the Quaker meeting had helped to ensure their survival through hard times when other non-conformist churches disappeared, but this concern for structure sometimes obscured the work of the Spirit, on which the business was based.

Residential Christian communities seemed to be springing-up all over the UK during the 1980's and three of us went to the first annual conference of the National Association of Christian Communities and Networks (NACCAN). When I told Rosalind Bellerby about this new association she responded by sending a cheque for £1,000 which helped NACCAN to become established. We added a further £100 and completed a long questionnaire about future possibilities. The Neighbours were to have a close association with NACCAN throughout its lifetime, until it came to an end in 2002.

A new resident in 1989 was Nina who was seriously anorexic and lived with us for over three years until 1992, sometimes deceiving us and the doctors by filling her pockets with stones when she went to be weighed and being unwilling to eat with us. At different times, Susan and Anne were her committed unofficial carers. They were patient with her to a fault but were sometimes tested to near despair by her behaviour. During the year she returned to hospital and nearly died of weight loss.

Martin, a young man with serious depression, who had come to live with the Halls at 148 in 1986, was a regular visitor for several years. He hanged himself in a local wood in 1990. Richard went to the inquest and and found it *a depressing occasion*.

So we came head-on with the trauma and distress caused by mental disorders and had no cause to be satisfied with our efforts to relieve the unhappiness of some of these young people. We realised how inadequate and under-funded was the NHS care for mental illness, the Cinderella of the health service. There are over a hundred minuted records of our discussions with and about the people we had living with us and we prayed together every morning.

### Year 7, 1990

The members at the beginning of the year were Anne, Michael, Susan, Roger, Jayne, Richard, and Claire.

In April 1990 for the first time we spent a Review Day at Turvey Abbey, a small Benedictine Monastery near Bedford and Susan wrote a perceptive report. Each member spoke about how they see the past and future of The Neighbours. Here are a few quotations:

' *A small sign of the Kingdom.'*

' *God's hand in my life.'*

' *To live simply; more sharing to see what might happen.'*

' *It takes a lot of energy, living together.'*

' *Get on and live together and no navel gazing'*

' *I am mystified that more people don't want to do the same thing.'*

Richard and Jayne emphasised that the energy required to keep The Neighbours on the road diverted energy from their local church. Claire wondered if the 'outside' common purpose of caring for people recovering from mental illness was the necessary glue to hold the Community together. She also spoke of the difficulties of being a single person in a community where the majority were married with family responsibilities. We ended with a time of worship including readings from Henri Nouwen and Michel Quoist. It was judged *a very good day* and it set a pattern of 'away-days' which continued for nearly twenty years.

Shortly after the Turvey day, Claire, with the blessing of the rest of the members, went to a convent in France for six months as 'time out' and possibly to test her vocation as to whether or not she was called to a vowed monastic life. The Neighbours Trust took on the renting of rooms at her house, 140, to enable her to continue to pay the mortgage, and a succession of young single people lived there over the summer months. Some took part in Neighbours events, others did not; some paid, others did not, leaving unpaid bills for rent and telephone. However, when Claire returned in December to resume her work and life in Northampton, the accounts showed a small surplus. We welcomed her back and she returned thanks for looking after the house. Some residents stayed on at 140 and there is reference to *Claire and her lost boys.*

Donald came to stay at 140 for a few months, *needing a place to be among caring people. Later he said 'The Neighbours gave me stability. I was able to join in without being under any pressure to*

*do so - Thursday supper, Saturday breakfast, Sunday tea. It was
a good space.'*

Meanwhile, at the other end of the houses, Richard had
been accepted for training for the Methodist ministry and
would need to move to Birmingham, to attend Queen's College.
Richard and Jayne accepted that we were all *bound together in the
property* and we searched for prospective members to buy 148
from them. At about this time Susan and I spent a week at the
Taizé Community with a group from Northampton churches
including John and Jenny Parkin whom we had known since
the visit of Virginia and Susan in 1988. John was a probation
officer of the old school, in close touch with his clients, mostly
young people in trouble with the law, and Jenny was a teacher.
After several discussions and a visit from their daughter Chloe
who asked to *drop-in* and have a look at us, they wrote to say
that *after a lot of prayer and discussion we would like to live at
148 and share the life of The Neighbours.* We welcomed them
and they put their house in Towcester on the market.

We had 148 valued and a price of £60,000 was initially agreed
by both parties; it was significant that this was three times the
price we had paid only seven years previously which indicated
the huge increases in house prices in the 1980s. First-time buyers
had the greatest difficulty in finding anything within their price
range and anyone who dropped out of house ownership during
this inflationary period would find it almost impossible to
return to it. However, there was a temporary seasonal fall in
prices during the winter months of 1991 and a revised price
of £57,500 was eventually agreed by *a sub-committee*. Richard
said they wanted all parties to regard the final outcome as a fair
deal. He noted that they seemed now to be selling during a dip
in the market whereas, if it had not been for the constraints of
The Neighbours agreement, they might have sold at a higher
price six months previously. We realised why most people
employed estate agents to do the bargaining (even for a 2½%
fee!) and we acknowledged and accepted the emotional risks of

direct negotiations. We thought that there was a fair chance that relationships *refined by fire* would thereby become stronger.

There always seem to be problems, both financial and emotional, with the buying and selling of houses, which perhaps is not surprising as these are usually the largest financial decisions that any of us make. In the special case of The Neighbours transactions, with the Agreements to consider, there were some awkward moments because of the unusual circumstances, but the main purpose of keeping the five houses intact when members moved on was achieved. The Agreements stipulated that leavers should give a year's notice to enable the remaining Members to find a buyer to join the community. If they failed to do so, the leaver was free to sell to anyone, on the open market. The community would have ended much earlier if this 12-month let-out clause had had to be activated but, in the event, all four sales during the life of the Community were to new Members.

The Halls moved to Birmingham in September to live for a time at the Ashram Community in Sparkbrook and reported that they were contributing *community-building skills using their experience at The Neighbours*. There were the usual and seemingly inevitable delays while the Parkins strove to sell their house in order to complete the purchase of 148 and enable the Halls to buy again. During this delay, frustrating for both families, the Halls rented 148 to the Clarke family who were in need of accommodation for a few months and it was March 1991 before the sales were completed and the Parkins were able to move in.

We had confirmed in December 1990 that renting residents in any of the houses should be invited to join prayers and community meals and other events, but should not be regarded as decision-making members due to the shorter term nature of their residence. The Members continued to be the house owners, each of whom was on the rota to lead prayers and take responsibility for the Community supper and meeting. This decision accounts for the varied handwriting and typing and styles of minute-taking which makes it quite a challenge for this author to decipher what was going on.

### Year 8, 1991

The members at the beginning of the year were Michael and Anne, Roger and Susan, Richard and Jayne, and Claire. Edith was living in the 144 flat.

We had spent some time on making rather complex and formal Agreements between the Joneses and Sawtells, with the Halls and with Claire to ensure that we could keep the five houses together. Bearing in mind the special problems with these 'restricted' sales we did not make a formal agreement with the Parkins or subsequent Members, but relied on the acceptance of Richard Hall's words that we were *bound together in the property*. This informal mutual trust rather than a formal signed Agreement thereafter seemed to us to be closer to the Gospel and, in due course, the two further house sales in 1998 went through on this basis. We asked potential members to think in terms of staying *not less than 2 years* as Members of the Community. This was not a burden as most house buyers would be thinking in longer terms and, in the event, all Members stayed four years or more and the average length of stay was ten years, which contributed significantly to the solidarity and continuity of the Community. Those who are renting, whether in a residential community or in open housing tend to move on at shorter intervals.

John and Jenny spoke of *the difficulties of dealing with two lots of people, Richard and Jayne selling the house and The Neighbours* concerned with potential community members. In retrospect, the problem of how to equate the need for community members to stay on the housing ladder with the necessity to keep the property intact for the Community to continue, was not solved, and stands in the way of new lay communities coming into being. Benedict had his own solution in the sixth century and the concept of celibate monks, taking lifetime vows and having no personal property, has endured down the centuries. We were searching for a way for unvowed lay people, married or single, sometimes with children, to live in community, not necessarily for their lifetime but maybe for a few years, as a part of their Christian witness. Benedict would probably say this was not possible. The Neighbours' experience was worth a try but it is perhaps unsurprising that few others have yet followed our pattern. Most members of Christian residential communities are renting not buying.

With regard to the common task, a huge amount of time and effort in 1991 was taken up with supporting Patrick and Nina both of whom were resident for the whole year. Patrick continued to hold down his job at the local NHS hospital but talked rather unrealistically about training as a radiologist. We considered he must move forward to a more self-supporting lifestyle but his financial situation was not good and Claire found it *not easy to extract money* from him for rent. As long as he took his correct medication he was all right, but he tended to vary the amount and this caused paranoiac episodes which were troubling both to him and to those of us around him.

Nina had returned from her eight month spell at St Crispin's Hospital in April 1990 and was struggling to maintain or increase her weight to a normal level. Week after week the minutes record the plans and agreements to help her, sometimes with her co-operation and sometimes her manipulative opposition. Sometimes we despaired of her ever moving on and we knew of sufferers from anorexia who had died rather than increase weight. She found it impossible to eat with us for most of the year and sat by herself in the kitchen. Occasionally she would join in but usually she was *round the corner* on her own but sometimes *with us in spirit*. Her boyfriend, Josh, was tireless in helping her and though he never lived in the Community we invited him to join the rota for leading morning prayers.

Since 1990 we had been in touch with a young man, Pablo, suffering from schizophrenia and he was a regular visitor at 140. We had no space for him to live with us and he was in and out of St. Andrew's Hospital, including two suicide attempts. Late one night in November 1991 at 140, after the others had gone to bed, he was in the living room and it seems he had been sniffing a liquid used for cleaning records. He was found to be dead. Possibly he had also taken some narcotic drug and we never knew for sure whether his death was misadventure or suicide. The minutes record, *We remember him as a charming handsome young man*, but this unhappy incident reminded us of the vulnerability of those to whom we offered support.

In November 1991 Susan and I set off on a journey *to visit several faraway friends and see what kind of world we live in, by travelling right round it..... we can report, surprise, surprise, that the world is amazing, beautiful, awe-inspiring, God-given and sometimes seemingly God-forsaken.* This quote is from our Christmas letter was written in December from New Zealand, where Susan's grandparents had briefly emigrated in the 1920s. We moved on to Australia and spent Christmas with friends in the Blue Mountains near Sydney and visited some of my distant relatives in Adelaide. My great-grandfather had emigrated there in the nineteenth century and started an optician's business. The sign SAWTELL was still above the shop and we were welcomed by 'the last Sawtell in the business'. We flew home on New Year's Day 1992.

### Year 9, 1992

The members throughout 1992 were Michael, Anne, Roger, Susan, John, Jenny, Claire and there were several renting residents.

In April, Susan and I went to Woodbrooke, the Quaker study centre in Birmingham where we had been invited to spend the summer term as Friends in Residence, to be part of the residential community there and teach a course on Christian

Communities. A beautiful place and a rewarding time which put us in touch with people from all over the world, studying at the Selly Oak colleges of which Woodbrooke was a part. We were away for four months, returning in July. At Woodbrooke, we met Andrew Nash, a Quaker, and he came came to live at 146 in September 1992 and stayed for over a year. He was a copy editor working from home in our dining room and took an active part in Neighbours events, including leading prayers from time to time. In 1994 he moved on to live at Llanerchwen, a retreat centre near Brecon.

In February we invited Adrian Smith of Movement for a Better World to co-ordinate our second Review Day and this turned out to be a programmed attempt to develop the Community and review progress on a regular basis. For the first time, we agreed the Purpose which is set out on page 16, and we listed the essential characteristics and issues. After eight years' community life we had gained confidence and organised a number of events in Christian Community Week in June. We identified a total of 29 residential Christian communities in the Northampton area, most of which were interdenominational. Some were 'enclosed' such as Turvey Monastery and others were 'open' like The Neighbours. We co-ordinated visits during the week and most of us spoke at meetings around the town churches.

In October we were also much involved with the annual NACCAN Assembly in Birmingham, which brought together people from about 60 residential communities and similar groups from all over the UK. All seven of us were there, Claire and Jenny led prayers and circle dancing. The chair of NACCAN thanked '*all of The Neighbours who gave so much time and energy to the Assembly. It was a very good day*. I recollect that the evening dancing got quite wild and a nun was whirling round so that her pendant crucifix was in danger of scything anyone nearby, like the swords on the wheels of Boudicca's chariot.

In November 1992 we went to Turvey again for another Review Day and discussed *hospitality*, the need for *rest, space and quality time* and policy for our supportive role ...*when inviting people with problems, such as mental illness, to stay in our homes, we should discuss this and gain the consent of the whole of the Neighbours.* We may not have realised at the time that this minute would lead to a significant turning point in 1993.

The behaviour of some of the residents tried us sorely and we seem to have had a lot of meetings at this time which sometimes led to sharp differences of opinions. For example, a rare event is recorded in September... *Roger apologised for proposing a change of meeting date. He admitted that this was an error of judgement on his part.*

Dozens of Minutes report our problems of trying to support Nina in her struggle to gain weight to enable her to live a more rewarding life. The plan was that she should gradually move to Josh's house in Wycliffe Road, five minutes' walk away, and take more responsibility for herself. We kept the room for her in 144 and she moved between the two, usually eating in 142 kitchen under Anne's eye. Eventually, in October, we agreed with her to regard Wycliffe Road as her home and she cleared her room at the Neighbours after three and half turbulent years. At least she was alive and a better weight but we *noted with sadness* her leaving letter which was negative and critical of our efforts to help her regain health. She continued to get better and in due course returned to university and was awarded a First Class degree in geography. She married the patient Josh and they have three children. Wonderful, Alleluia! She declined to keep in touch with us after she left and perhaps this is understandable as we represented a very difficult period of her life which she may want to forget. We know this is a well-known syndrome and we have experience of people who survived terrifying wartime experiences but never spoke of it for years afterwards. We regretted that The Neighbours experience had been so horrible for Nina, rejoiced at her recovery, and accepted her wish to put this part of her life behind her. However, the scars remain with some of those who cared for her.

Patrick also moved out during the year to share a house with a friend in Wellingborough, but then asked to return and was still with us at the year end. Here again the Minutes are packed with reports of many discussions and plans to help him take his medication to minimise the paranoia which often beset him. He showed considerable determination to retain his portering job at the local NHS Hospital and is rightly proud of his employment there over a long period. He said *how much he valued the support of The Neighbours in helping him overcome his mental illness and hold down a permanent job. He says he has come to see The Neighbours as his second family*. All of us in some degree, but Claire in particular, helped him towards a less dependent lifestyle.

The problems of house ownership were frequently debated during 1991 and we learned from the procedure of the Hall/Parkin sale. We decided to cancel the earlier Agreements and adopt what we termed, rather grandly, a Deed of Mutual Covenant which was signed by the seven of us on 23 July 1992. The Preamble states that *The Neighbours is an act of faith and therefore most decisions should not be taken in advance but only when they become topical. Nevertheless, one significant matter which needs to be clear to us in advance is the procedure by which members may leave the project and dispose of their house*. The Covenant then details the selling/buying procedure which was put into effect in 1993 (Jones/Tickle) and twice in 1998 (Parkin/Frier and Caddick/Tickle). Benedict and most subsequent monastic orders with life vows, do not have this problem as the assumption is that monks will never need to own property again. However, we are aware that it is not any longer infrequent for such monastic life vows to be discontinued and we know one or two people who have left monastic orders and faced considerable problems in finding accommodation.

During the year we settled into a rota for leading Community morning prayers and a friend commented that we were '*a church which meets every day except Sundays*'. The weekday pattern was about twenty minutes and on Saturdays we invited friends to join us for a rather longer worship time followed by breakfast together.

On Sunday afternoons we had an open tea in the Neighbours Room at 144, to which half a dozen regulars came, and followed it during Lent with an evening prayer in the style of Taizé and a bring-and-share supper afterwards.

The Neighbours Meeting every Thursday evening alternated between 'business' one week and 'bible study' the other, a deliberate 'Martha and Mary' pattern which we continued for years. For the study evening, we considered whether or not to look at *Community and Growth* by Jean Vanier (Revised Edition, Paulist Press 1989) the founder of L'Arche and a towering figure in the world of Christian communities. We regarded it as the best book dealing with our concerns but a whimsical Minute reads *Agreed to stay with the Bible rather than other holy books*.

We used The Neighbours Trust to receive rent from residents and contributions from the various groups using the Neighbours Room and we paid out from it any expenses which were agreed to be community concerns rather than individual household ones, such as donations to Emmaus for providing lunch for Nina and to Movement for a Better World for Adrian Smith's work with us at the February review day. The assets of the Trust at the year-end were £9,421 but in subsequent years this figure gradually diminished.

The five narrow gardens converted into one large square garden took up a lot of energy. Michael grew flowers and shrubs and John concentrated on vegetables which we all ate with enthusiasm. However, the garden needed a good deal of maintenance and in June, *John had been unwell for a little while … and help would be welcomed*. This must have been forthcoming because in August he was picking grapes, no less, in the 142 conservatory.

1992 was a year of considerable Community activity and outreach. We had grown in confidence about what we were doing and we were increasingly asked to share our experience with others. Perhaps this was a high point in the development of small residential Christian communities nationally as well as at The Neighbours.

### Year 10, 1993

Members at the beginning of the year were Michael, Anne, Roger, Susan, Claire, John, Jenny. Edith was living in the 144 flat and there were several residents in need of some support.

NACCAN published a Directory of Christian Groups, Communities and Networks from time to time and the Third Edition in 1993 lists 85 residential Christian communities in UK. These were lay communities rather than monastic ones and we began to receive numerous visitors wanting to discuss aspects of community living. Richard Grover came from a similar project in north London, Chris Lawson and a delegation from Woodbrooke, the Quaker Study Centre in Birmingham, Steve and Denise Summers who subsequently were founding members of a community project in Hood Street, about a mile away from The Neighbours.

After the 1992 optimism, 1993 turned out to be an unsettled year during which we had many discussions about how the Community might develop, particularly in respect of our adopted task of offering supportive accommodation to people with mental health problems.

Patrick moved from 140 to 142 in June 1993 and continued to live in the Community for the rest of the year. We encouraged him to move on as soon as he could find an appropriate place and agreed to continue to give him whatever support we could, once he had moved. Michael and Anne in particular have offered him open hospitality during all the ensuing years as he moved from one place to another.

We made no claims to be professionals in dealing with mental illness but we were aware that the psychiatric services available on the NHS in the town were pitifully inadequate for the needs of people discharged from hospital. Due to the slur of mental illness parents did not always welcome back their young people and thus they were marooned in Northampton with nowhere to live, either supported or unsupported. We knew at least one father who refused to allow his son to come home. We considered that, as a group of Christians committed to Gospel values of compassion for those in need, we should be able to *make a difference*, but we were aware of the difficulties. In 1992 two of the young men with whom we had been in touch for some years, had killed themselves because they could see no way forward. The protracted and unhappy ending of our three-and-a-half year journey with Nina had left us troubled and uncertain about what we were attempting.

In 1993, two of the members of The Neighbours were probation officers and another was a teacher. As part of their work, they were dealing with people with serious social problems and found it difficult to return home after a strenuous day's work to find similar problems round the supper table. Four of the members, Michael and Anne, Susan and me, were retired and had the time and energy to give to supporting the people living with us, but some members expressed the view that the kind of help we were able to give was insufficient for their complex needs and we should be more active in encouraging them into independent living in order to grow and flourish.

These tensions came to a head over the matter of Jean, recently discharged from hospital where she had been treated for depression. She asked if we could offer her a room as she had no home. At a long and unhappy meeting on 4 March each of us expressed our views on whether or not we should continue to offer supportive accommodation. No decision was recorded.

After the meeting, Michael and Anne decided to offer Jean a room in their house, independently of the Community. Before they had had an opportunity to report this to other members, as they were away for the weekend, Jean appeared on the doorstep with her suitcase. I answered the door, was surprised to see her, and had to tell her that we had made no decision and could not give her a room. She was distressed and said that Michael and Anne had invited her. I said I was not aware of that and we compromised by paying for her to stay at a local bed & breakfast.

On their return, Michael and Anne were angered that I had turned Jean away and said they were entitled to invite whoever they wished to stay in their house. Long before the emergence of The Neighbours Community they had opened their house to all manner of needy people and such hospitality had become for them a wonderful ministry. They pointed out that we had deliberately taken on this supportive role and we should not turn Jean away, but on 25 March we spent a further hour in discussion and agreed the minute, *We do not plan to offer accommodation to additional people recovering from mental illness, at present. We shall continue to offer hospitality*. I recollect that my view was that, however inadequate, our residential support was worthwhile because there was nowhere else for them to go. However, Susan and I were aware that we could only continue this task if members were united and as this was not the case, I agreed with the proposal that we should discontinue it.

In retrospect this apparently small event was a turning point for the Community, one of only a few during a quarter of a century. It was a failure of communication but also a sharp reminder of the hazards of community living and the difficulty of finding a balance between family autonomy and the agreed common task of the community. Michael and Anne who have been hugely hospitable throughout their married life were not happy with the decision to discontinue and this incident contributed towards them, on 27 April 1993, giving a formal year's notice to leave the Community as required by the Deed of Mutual Covenant. As fellow founder members, this came as a serious blow to Susan and me and I wondered if it would be the end of the Community, especially as we knew of other Christian residential groups which had foundered and ended unhappily because of similar disagreements about common purpose. However, The Neighbours weathered this storm and we refused to allow it to break the friendships between us. Writing twenty years after these events Susan and I retain our friendships with all the members of the Community and continue to go walking with Michael and Anne each month. We are also in touch with several of the young men who stayed with us, who look back on their time at The Neighbours as a helpful contribution to their return to more independent living.

After this painful debate, we continued to offer support to a number of non-residents but we gradually reduced the residential supportive role and replaced it with other tasks such as sustaining members working in demanding situations, organising quiet days, creative mornings and hospitality on a daytime basis

For example, Thomas, who was in and out of hospital coping with schizophrenia, appears in the Minutes over several years. In March it was reported that he *was on new medication and verbally abusive ... it would be unwise to allow him* to come into any of our houses. However, it seems we persevered because in August it was agreed to make him a holiday grant of £200 from the Trust. I went with him for a bizarre weekend holiday in Blackpool where his strange behaviour was very puzzling to our seaside boarding house landlady. We went to the zoo where Thomas made faces at the animals. I was reminded of Stanley Holloway's monologue, *Albert and the Lion*, where young Albert, visiting Blackpool with his dad, was disappointed that *'there was no wrecks nor anyone drownded, in fact nothing to laugh at all ... so they paid and went into the zoo'*. Fortunately

Thomas did not tease the lions, like Albert, who got eaten by one of them. Thomas now (2014) lives in a residential care home in Northampton and I see him from time to time. Our friendship has lasted for over thirty years.

The members during the ensuing thirteen years of the life of the Community adopted this changed focus from residential to non-residential support. For example, Richard Appleby was manager of the local soup kitchen, dealing with a demanding clientele and Pam used her gifts as a painter and teacher to organise Open Days.

In May 1993, at a review of our morning prayer pattern, we agreed that we *would like more silence … and shorter readings.* Perhaps this was due to having two Quakers on the rota, but in December words were back in fashion because Anne and Susan prepared an advent liturgy with responses. Each of us was asked to bring something of significance and these included *a packet of seeds, an Iona prayer, a brick, a Taizé song, a picture of the earth from the moon', and even a file of early Neighbours Minutes.* Now I wonder who could have brought that?

John and Jenny Parkin were keen gardeners and Michael was pleased to have more help. In July, *John reported sweet peas, French beans, courgettes and cucumbers* were all available. Jenny fell into the pond during enthusiastic efforts to introduce fish which were to be fed by Edith. There were other pond casualties from time to time, including Susan's cousin who fell in, cold-stone sober, during a family party and had to be kitted out in my spare trousers which were several sizes too large for him. I was concerned that he might trip over them and be immersed again, but he survived without further mishap.

The change of focus caused us to re-evaluate The Neighbours Trust and after several discussions we separated the Trust from the Community and renamed it The Neighbours Mental Health Trust (TNMHT). The assets at this transfer were £9,500 and we widened the scope in order to make grants to people with whom we were in touch, not necessarily living at The Neighbours.

The community finances continued as the Common Fund to which each household made a contribution and the fund paid out corporate expenses such as the garden and the upkeep of the Neighbours Room. *Roger will deal with these administrative changes* and I reported in September that the Common Fund stood at £140 and was kept in a tin box in the 146 cellar. This tin continued in service for the following fourteen years.

TNMHT gradually acquired a life of its own, independent of the Community. In 2007 the fund stood at over £10,000 and the remaining Trustees, Michael, Anne, Susan and myself, decided to give it a new focus. I had been the administrator and secretary for twenty years and now handed over to Michael. We decided to give £1,000 block grants to three people who were in day to day contact with mental illness, either in hospital or in the community, to enable them to make individual grants whenever needed without the chore of bringing each case to the Trustees.

In this way, a lay member of the Chaplaincy team at the NHS psychiatric hospital was able to make immediate small grants to patients, so was the manager of MIND (Northampton) and also a social worker attached to Maple Access, a town centre doctor's practice which has a special role for people with mental disorders. Such grants might be for items of equipment like a new cooker or help towards a holiday, or whatever was the immediate need not met from elsewhere. Twice a year, the three grantees reported back to the Trustees and further block grants were agreed. This turned out to be a satisfactory way of using the Trust money and it continued for several years. By 2011 there was no money remaining in the Trust and we debated whether or not to close it. It was decided to keep it going on the same basis, with particular reference to Maple Access, the doctor's practice where Simon Tickle, a previous member of The Neighbours Community, was the senior partner. Dealing with patients struggling to get away from drug or alcohol addiction, it is a useful facility for the practice staff to have access to an independent fund from which small grants can be made

### Year 11, 1994
Members at the beginning of the year were Michael, Anne, Roger, Susan, Claire, John, Jenny. Edith was living in the 144 flat.

Deborah and Simon Tickle with their three children lived at Earls Barton where Simon was the local GP. They had shown an interest in The Neighbours soon after the community began and when Michael and Anne decide to move on they were happy to sell their house and buy 142 to join. From January 1994 onwards they came to the weekly meeting and on 5 May we had a party, including all the children, to say goodbye to Anne and Michael, Edith and Andrew, and to welcome Simon and Deborah. *Jenny will organise a beetle drive, Claire and Roger will each make a parcel for 'passing the parcel … Susan will make meringues.*

Deborah and Simon, with Emily, Clare, Joe, Ticker the cat and Fred the hamster, moved into 142 the day after Michael and Anne and Edith moved out. A minute notes that this reduced the average age of people living at The Neighbours, including children, from 54 to 33. Deborah came from a Baptist background and Simon was an active Roman Catholic, so they had no problem in joining an interdenominational community and soon became involved in all aspects of what we were doing. Simon replaced Michael as 'head gardener' and produced a three-page garden plan, some of which happened.

In place of Edith, we let the 144 flat to Moyna Antill, who had been living in one of the community houses of the Jesus Fellowship. We hoped that she would become an active member of The Neighbours and although she did take part in some events, came occasionally to prayers and ran a children's crèche at a Community Gathering, she felt unable to become a fully-participating member and lived a rather separate life.

We considered making the flat more self-contained for her by putting in a spiral staircase but there was not enough room for it and so she had to share our staircase at 146. She needed to give priority of time and energy to her work as a classroom assistant at a special school in Kettering and this enabled her to pay the rent and live an independent life throughout all the nine years she was with us, before she returned to live with her parents in 2003. We continue to keep in touch with her and rejoice that she is taking courses to qualify for promotion in her work.

Patrick had moved on again in March, after over six years with us, to live a more independent life but has always kept in touch with Michael and Anne, and with Susan and me. For some years he has lived in his own flat, with some background support, and held on to his work as a porter at the local NHS hospital, surviving several re-organisations.

Thereafter we did not have any people recovering from mental illness living with us for the thirteen following years of the Community, but we continued to be in touch with a handful of 'day visitors', particularly for Sunday tea.

During the year we had numerous discussions about the purpose and procedures of the Community, wrestling with the differences between legal and moral agreements, the Deed of Mutual Covenant and the manner of taking decisions. At one stage we managed to follow the Quaker procedure of writing and agreeing the minutes at the meeting itself and we accepted that *there was no distinction between business and worship and that meetings ought to be held prayerfully*.

We decided to have an evening prayer every day from Monday to Friday for a trial period of a month but it seemed that this did not continue. We considered turning the 148 garage into a chapel or '*prayer shed*' but this did not happen either. However, we did write various liturgies for Community occasions and the prayer life of the Community was under regular discussion. (See Appendix D, An *Agape*.)

The Neighbours was beginning to be more widely known and we were asked to host a regional NACCAN meeting. Twenty-six people were present on 30 July and the large garden was ideal for a summer gathering. It was judged a useful occasion and a visitor wrote, '*I was very inspired to see your homes and gladdened to find out about a place that is living the ideal community. God bless you all*'. There was a certain irony in this and other similar comments as the minute book throughout the year indicates that the members were very unsure of the direction of the Community following the departure of Michael and Anne. We would not have claimed it to be the '*ideal community*'.

While we hesitated, others set out to replicate what we were doing. I was invited to talk to an interdenominational planning group in Milton Keynes, a 23 mile walk along the Grand Union canal, which in due course became The Well at Willen community, including Roman Catholics, Quakers and Anglicans.

Helping us in our debates was Michael Jackson, a Methodist minister who was spending a three-month sabbatical visiting a range of residential communities. He asked to join in our prayers and *open meetings* and became a friend whose insight has been valuable to us for over twenty years.

When Michael and Anne moved, Susan and I bought their share of 144 so that we owned the whole house and were able to let it, at cost, to the various households of the Community. Deborah and Simon rented the front bedroom which already had a connecting door to 142. The community paid a rent from the Common Fund for the Neighbours Room where The Order of St Luke prayer group for healing met every week for about fifteen years, mostly under the guidance of our friend Ken Thomason who, more than nearly anyone else of my acquaintance, lived by Jesus' teaching. A Weston Favell church planning group also met in the Neighbours Room, as did Daily Bread Co-operative members for an away-day in October. We were glad to have the room widely used and considered that this might be part of our common task, replacing the provision of supportive accommodation which we had now discontinued.

### Year 12, 1995

Members at the beginning of the year were, Roger, Susan, Claire, Jenny, John, Deborah, Simon. Moyna was living in the 144 flat.

Jenny led a discussion on making the Neighbours Room *more prayerful* and we agreed to remove the battered piano, box-in the fireplace and provide better facilities in the utility room next door. Susan and Jenny re-decorated the walls. The result was a less cluttered space and the room was widely used during the year. We were involved with the Abington/Weston Favell Ecumenical Lent Groups and invited the planning group to supper. Simon arranged for the Jabbok Theatre to give a performance and his doctor's surgery had their Christmas dinner there. We agreed for the room to be used for his grandmother's funeral service and a prayer group for healing met every week. We invited friends to join us for a Maundy Thursday *agape*.

The members met daily for morning prayers and on Saturdays we had a communal breakfast. Sunday tea had become a regular date for a handful of people with mental health problems. Without taking any formal decision, the administration of all these Neighbours Room activities became a major part of the outward task of the Community. A comfortable room in an ordinary street seemed to be a more attractive venue than a draughty church hall with locked cupboards, and we provided good Fairtrade coffee and a centrally-heated loo. Visiting groups added to the Common Fund by means of a collecting box left in a prominent place.

Janey O'Shea, Quaker Studies Tutor at Woodbrooke came to spend a day with us in March and we asked her to help us: *to affirm our gifts as individuals ... to build-up whatever corporate truth is appropriate for The Neighbours ... to discuss how we might express this in our prayer together.*

I thought we might have found a new direction for the Community and was saddened when Claire told us that she *had been feeling unsettled for some time* and asked not to be considered a member but had no definite plans for the future. Simon drafted a healing/reconciliation service and we had several discussions without coming to any decisions except to agree that we should accept that Claire should continue to live at 140 if she wished to do so, but would no longer be on any of the rotas for prayers, meals etc. We asked John to discuss with her the feelings of the other members and to keep in touch with her. Later in the year there was a happier minute: *All very glad to hear that Claire and Chris are to be married on 28 December. She has asked to discuss the future with The Neighbours*'. Some of us went to their lovely wedding at Maldon, with the reception on a Thames barge.

One door closes but another one opens. On 30 March, *All present except for Deborah!! Rowan was born yesterday*. Great rejoicing and before long Deborah was mowing the lawn with the baby on her back, African style. Rowan was christened in September; twenty-five people for lunch in the Neighbours Room and 100 at the service in the afternoon. The Neighbours 'choir' rendered *A Touching Place. All agreed a truly sacramental occasion.*

In May, Jeanne Hinton, working for the World Council of Churches, came to stay for a week to gather material for a case study of The Neighbours which she completed in 1996. Jeanne is a writer and a sympathetic observer rather than a member, so her study of the first twelve years of the Community is more objective than mine. A copy is attached to Minute Book Volume 7. On the cover she quotes Susan saying, '*It was important to us that we find a way of being together that was not radically different from the way others live, but that enabled us to pray* together daily, to do some things together and to support one another. *The sort of community that can happen anywhere.'*

John said *opt for the joyous* and celebrated his fiftieth birthday in August with a party in a large marquee on the lawn. He also gave notice that he was going to Ruskin College, Oxford, for the autumn term and Jenny was starting her training for the Anglican priesthood.

An unusual visitor at this time was Peter who had no home and moved about the country from place to place. A dreamy quiet young man, he asked permission to sleep in the 146 garage and made no further request for food or shelter. To earn his keep he made insoles for shoes and I still have a pair. We glimpsed him coming and going from time to time during the summer, until he disappeared and we have never heard tell of him since. Peter was a welcome guest but we also had a number of more difficult ones. The word got around that The Neighbours had a concern for people recovering from mental illness and it was not unusual to receive letters or phone calls from people wanting to join us. We soon realised that there were some people with huge emotional needs who moved from one residential community to another and our ability to meet those needs was limited. Their concern was 'What can this community do for me?' but as we began to recognise the category, our first question was 'What can you contribute to the life of this community?' Monastic orders have the same problem and the word 'gyrovague', which sounds like a helicopter, is described as 'a wandering and usually dissolute monk of the early Church'. Our wandering visitors were seldom dissolute, but they were needy, and we realised that there are very few places to go for patients discharged from psychiatric hospitals, when often they have been rejected by their families. Benedictine Rule LXI 'How Travelling Monks are to be received' addresses this problem in wonderful language:

If a travelling monk should arrive from some far-off locality, and want to live as a guest in the monastery, and be content with the customs he finds there, and not disturb the community by making special demands, let him be accepted for as long as he desires. And if indeed with humble charity he reasonably criticises or points some things out, the Abbot should consider the matter carefully. For it may be that the Lord has sent him for this very purpose … If on the other hand he should be found demanding or a man of bad habits, not only should he not be allowed to join the community but he should be frankly told to go away, for fear that others should be corrupted by his unhappy condition. (*The Rule of St Benedict*, Abbot Parry (Gracewing 1990))

I am in no doubt that there were people who '*the Lord has sent*' to our community, but there were others who were '*found demanding*'.

On a sunny October Saturday we organised another Community Gathering in association with NACCAN, for information, discussion and prayer. Over forty people came for a bring-and-share lunch and Jenny led a prayer in the style of Taizé. A discussion about celebrating the Eucharist in a residential community led to the comment, *we want to celebrate Holy Communion with each other, to share it and do it ourselves. Philip said, 'At Daily Bread usually there is a minister present but from time to time a lay person has presided and this has seemed to be acceptable'.*

### Year 13, 1996

Members at the beginning of the year were Susan, Roger, Jenny, John, Deborah, Simon. Claire and Chris were living at 140 and Moyna at 144.

To keep in touch with Claire and Chris, it was agreed to *share a meal … once a month*. Chris, who is an architect, drew a huge comprehensive plan of the garden and worked with Simon to re-shape some areas. We all had ideas about the pond, how to encourage fish but prevent the children from falling in; however, most of the fish died and children continued to fall in from time to time. Chris celebrated his fortieth birthday with a party in the garden in August and Claire was happily pregnant. In due course we welcomed the arrival of Dominic.

Meetings were rather sporadic and we *abandoned* the Quaker practice of writing the minutes and agreeing them before closing the meeting. I think we found this too difficult. The Common Fund fell into arrears as members did not all pay their contributions. *We decided to operate on a 'faith basis', i.e. we will not make any assessments but wait in confidence for contributions to the Fund.* This appeared to work as the annual accounts showed a credit balance in the tin in the 146 cellar, helped by £242 from the St Luke's group during the year.

Surprisingly it was only in 1996 that we decided to use the 'new version' of the Lord's Prayer. Susan was thanked for assembling the Psalms from the New Zealand Prayer Book and we had ten copies made of this version for daily use. *We will not use the John Wesley pause* when reading the Psalms at morning prayers. Now that most of the Tickle children were school age, we formed a 'worship sub-committee' consisting of Simon, Jenny, Roger, to plan a crib service at Christmas and to *try to keep the ... prayers child-friendly.*

Jenny rounded off a meeting in March by leading a circle dance rehearsal which resulted in *everyone getting into a circular arm-lock. Deborah demonstrated some impossible yoga positions.*

We kept in touch with the emerging Christian community in Hood Street and joined them for circle dancing on a Sunday afternoon later in the year.

A strange minute in May reads, *Hair. Jenny to ring Sharon to do Chloe and Roger in addition to herself on 3 June.*

We were not happy with the weekly meetings. Susan had suggested earlier that *we should invite Moyna to come to the meetings which Claire and Chris attend, to encourage more community spirit and communications.* Maybe hair was under control but a draft minute in October drew further attention to our problems: *Jenny has asked us to review our meals and meetings. She had felt the pressure of meetings weighing on her. In various ways most of us expressed similar feelings of … staleness, drifting … and wasted opportunity.* She had started a placement at St Alban's Church in September as part of her training for ordination and knew that she and John would need to move on when she was ordained and assigned to a parish.

We went as a group to an inter-faith interdenominational celebration at Turvey Abbey, our local Benedictine monastery, but found it *a little disappointing.* This was surprising because the monks and nuns of Turvey were a wonderful resource to us over a period of twenty years.

Another strange minute appears in October. Apparently I had been investigating the import of loofahs with a view to selling them at Daily Bread Co-operative as pan scourers as well as back scourers. *Roger's loofah survey was somewhat negative. However, Simon found loofahs excellent for demonstrating osteoporosis.*

The crib service before Christmas included a stunning performance by Emily Tickle as the inn-keepers son:

> 'I was mucking out the stables when this bloke came along knocking on everybody's doors, saying ' Can I sleep here?' At last he came to us.

> I watched amazed as Dad said he could sleep in our stable with his pregnant wife! I was flabbergasted and I froze in shock. My Dad - kind! Whoa!

> The lady was very quiet but her husband kept asking for water for her. At last the baby was born and I went into the stable and I saw these three (rich) men and some

shepherds. I told them to get lost! But Mary said she wanted them to stay.

Then I saw a load of weirdos flying in the sky – I'm seeing illusions – so I went to the doctor's. He says 'Have you seen a psychiatrist?' And I said 'No, only angels.'

Well, the next day the guests in our stable left for Egypt. A few hours after they'd gone a lady called Babushka came along and asked to see the baby.

I go, 'Oi, first three men come saying they're from the Far East and now you come. Don't tell me … you walked all the way from Russia to see a baby.'

### Year 14, 1997
Members in residence at the beginning of the year were Roger, Susan, John, Jenny, Deborah, Simon. Moyna was living at 144 and Chris and Claire at 140.

In community terms, 1996 had been a low key year and it came as no surprise that in January 1997 both John and Jenny and Claire and Chris gave a year's notice of moving on. Jenny and John expected to move into parish accommodation in 1998 and Chris expected to be made redundant in 1998 and was considering the possibility of becoming a self-employed architect in Exeter, his home city.

A year seemed a long time to be in limbo but we knew from experience that it takes time to find people choosing to make the move from independent to community living and so it proved in 1997. The task fell to the remaining four members, Deborah and Simon, Susan and me. We sent out a letter to sixty people, headed *seeking a shared lifestyle* and adopted the descriptive phrase *A Community of Households*. It included, after thirteen years, a statement of purpose!

The purpose of The Neighbours is to develop a community life which enables us to explore and share our faith and care for others according to the Gospel. Our wider aims are to encourage Christian unity and to seek understanding with those of different faiths.

There was a heart-warming response to this circular and we spent the rest of the year corresponding and discussing with enquirers of all shapes and sizes, quite a demanding experience, but useful, as we needed to be clear about our purpose and realistic about the problems and the benefits.

We were aware that the complex agreements we had made in 1993 regarding the procedure for selling and buying any of the five community houses, were unlikely to make a smooth passage for these transactions which were nearly every household's primary financial commitment. The problem was that if the community was to continue, we could not allow estate agents to find prospective buyers on the open market to enable the sellers to accept the highest bid, but the sellers, John and Jenny, Claire and Chris, would be buying on the open market and therefore needed to sell at the best price. In other words, we were looking to make a private sale, without involving estate agents, but at the market price which was reckoned to be £75,000 for 148 and £71,000 for 140. A tortuous procedural Amendment we had made in 1993 regarding the procedure for selling proved to be impractical and it was agreed in November to withdraw it and enable the sellers *to negotiate with potential buyers in whatever manner they chose, to bring about a settlement acceptable to buyer and seller.* We succeeded in the sense that both houses were handed on to people who came in order to become community members, but there were some traumatic moments in the process.

After her husband died, Pam Frier had made her house in Surrey into a House of Prayer and wanted to do something similar if she came to Northampton. We discussed with her and agreed, *Pam would like to use 148 for quiet days/creativity days/spiritual accompaniment. We accepted this as part of our collective vision and would regard it as a Neighbours ecumenical project to which we will all contribute.* So we invited her to join the Neighbours and after some time of thought and prayer, she accepted and agreed a price with John and Jenny without recourse to estate agents.

At the other end of the five houses we had known the Appleby family for some time. Richard was manager of the Northampton soup kitchen where I was a Sunday volunteer, and Patricia was looking after their four children, the youngest of whom had suffered serious burns in a domestic accident. They were members of the congregation at the Roman Catholic Cathedral in the town. They needed a secure home and wanted to be part of The Neighbours but did not own a house to sell and their credit rating was insufficient for them to obtain a mortgage to buy 140.

At the same time as these discussions were happening, on behalf of the community, I was investigating the possibility of forming a housing co-operative to take on the ownership of some of the five houses and simplify the ownership arrangements. I got as far as completing a set of Model Rules which could be used by other NACCAN communities in similar situations, but there were too many unsolved problems and so eventually the idea of a co-operative was abandoned. There was not much interest from the other Neighbours and I think it was regarded as *one of Roger's hare-brained schemes to turn the world upside down overnight.* The world of property ownership, particularly in the Thatcher era of the 1990s, was not for turning.

To rub salt into my unjustified wounded pride and as an ironic reinforcement of the importance of property, we were requested to pay £5 towards the administration of a Neighbourhood Watch scheme for Ardington Road and we agreed *as a mark of solidarity though we have reservations about the organisation.*

The Neighbours Room continued to be widely used by ourselves and by outside groups. Deborah and Simon ran a marriage preparation group under the auspices of the Roman Catholic organisation, Teams of Our Lady, and the priest in charge at the Cathedral, Ken Payne, became a long-term friend of the community. We organised a number of prayers in the style of Taizé and were actively involved with Churches Together in Northampton as part of our commitment to Christian unity. We also took part in NACCAN Exchange Week: *Simon and Deborah would like to visit another community such as Orthona or Bruderhof. Their house would be available to incoming visitors.* Four of us went to the annual NACCAN Assembly in Birmingham and *Susan led a Lectio Divina on Isaiah 49.*

The garden was also well used. *John assisted by Claire* grew vegetables and salad stuff in the greenhouse. Deborah was in charge of grass-cutting and I looked after the garbage and compost bins. Claire put up an outside playpen to keep Dominic away from the pond. A special event for Susan and me was a summer party in a marquee in the garden to celebrate our 40th. wedding anniversary. People were asked to take us as they found us and *We will not make any exceptional effort to weed or tidy.* A hundred and twenty friends and relations came, from far and wide, and the sun shone.

### Year 15, 1998

Members at the beginning of the year were Susan, Roger, John, Jenny, Simon, Deborah. Moyna was living at 144.

Claire needed to sell 140 with minimum delay as she and Chris were moving to Exeter. After much discussion of alternative solutions, we agreed that five of us (Simon, Deborah, Roger, Susan, Pam) should put up £15,000 each and Simon and Deborah should become the owners for the time being, holding the house '*upon trust*'. Richard and Patricia were encouraged to buy the house from us as soon as they could get a mortgage. We recorded these arrangements with a formal Agreement and

Declaration of Trust but did not consider that we needed to employ a solicitor as there was a strong element of mutual trust between the community members. Richard and Patricia with Matthew, Sarah, Chris and Jonathan moved into 140 in April 1998 and paid a spasmodic rent.

We had *A Special Day*, at John and Jenny's suggestion, to celebrate *the new Neighbours* with a reading from Genesis 28. It was a different community because there would now be eight children, four Tickles and four Applebys, as well as seven adult members. On Maundy Thursday, *we had an ecumenical* agape *supper* with all the children present and taking part, lighting candles, breaking bread and singing *O let all who thirst, let them come*. We had a farewell supper with John and Jenny in May and Jenny was thrilled that we all went to her ordination at Peterborough Cathedral.

Pam moved into 148 in June 1998 and remained a member of the community for nine years, continuing to live in the house after the community ended in 2007.

This change of composition took time to settle and there were some strange episodes. Matthew Appleby said he had heard a rumour that no TV was allowed in the Community and although he soon found that this was not the case, he proceeded to play loud music in his bedroom so that relations with the folk next door at 138 were somewhat strained, to put it mildly. Initially we refused his request for him and his friends to camp in the garden but when *he expressed disappointment with the decision* we allowed his appeal and with some nervous anticipation gave him permission. Matthew was testing the boundaries of this strange community. There were several shouting matches on the doorstep but Simon exercised his peace-making skills and violence was avoided. In the garden it was suggested we needed more shrubs *to resist footballs*.

At the same time, Pam began to initiate children's activities with clay modelling and painting events for the Neighbours children and others too. Our grandchildren enjoyed getting their hands into the clay.

It was not all noise as Pam soon organised her first Quiet Day to which 16 people came and these days became a significant part of our outreach over the next few years. Morning prayers continued as before and on Thursday evenings each of us in turn reported on our spiritual journeys. Patricia reports *a very enriching evening*. During Advent we tried a voluntary evening prayer at 9.15pm but there was not much response.

The enabling committee of Churches Together in Northampton (CTN) met in the Neighbours Room to plan a huge event in Abington Park for Pentecost 2000. I was involved and asked the community to make a special donation for this event but some *spoke against, reflecting that giving to alleviate famine in Sudan should take preference over UK Millennium celebrations. The matter was deferred until the 146 household had got its act together*. I do not recollect the outcome but we organised a coffee morning in October for the Save the Children Appeal for famine relief in Sudan. Some situations are slow to change; thirteen years earlier, in 1985, our daughter Mary, had been working with Save the Children at Safawa refugee camp on the border of Sudan and Ethiopia, helping to feed starving children.

Richard organised a Caribbean Evening in the garden on a summer evening, to raise funds for the soup kitchen. He expected about 50 people but nearly 100 came and the steel band made a loud noise far into the night. Fortunately we had specifically invited all the nearby neighbours but we did get some complaints from further up the road. Simon's peace-making skills were again employed and an angry letter segued into a friendly relationship in due course.

Another noisy event was a charismatic healing group meeting in the Neighbours Room in the evening. There was concern that the children would not get to sleep because the leader explained that *sometimes they would have to shout in their ministry and sing in tongues. We did not feel we should be judgemental about this but asked them to sing early rather than late.*

We asked Sarah Appleby to make a survey of what activities the community children would welcome and a long list included face painting and badger watching. There were sixteen present for baked beans and bangers on 5 November followed by a *huge bonfire*. Matthew enjoyed himself and *masterminded a firework display – no casualties*. Later in November we joined up with two other Christian communities, Hood Street and The Well at Willen for a day together, with circle dancing and discussion of *What's the Vision?*

The link with Daily Bread Co-operative continued, with combined carol singing and we had a Christmas *agape*, including the children, but decided to discontinue the weekly outreach Sunday tea after about ten years.

With three members leaving and three new ones joining, 1998 was a year of change. Having had no school age children until 1994, we now had eight so they outnumbered the adult members and influenced whatever we did as a community.

### Year 16, 1999
At the beginning of the year the members were Susan, Roger, Deborah, Simon, Patricia, Richard, Pam. Moyna was living at 144.

The new members were finding their feet and we gradually agreed that hospitality to individuals and groups was the new common task and, for the first time, we published a programme of events with a new strap-line – *THE NEIGHBOURS – an ecumenical community of households*. The programme included *Agape* lunches, Days of Stillness, Bible Sharing in the manner of Quakers, prayers in the manner of Taizé.

In April, people from eight local residential and working Christian communities came to a day event, in association with NACCAN, including our friends Brother John and Brother Herbert from the Benedictine monastery at Turvey.

We calculated that the 28 people present had *over 100 years of community experience in the Northampton area, but unsurprisingly, none claimed to have the whole truth or the perfect community lifestyle. We celebrated our unity in the Gospel and came to a better understanding of our diversity. It was an occasion of friendship and solidarity.*

In October we welcomed a group of eighteen priests from France, led by Ken Payne from the Roman Catholic Cathedral in Northampton. They said: *Un grand merci de la part de tous les prêtres*, or something similar.

Several groups met regularly in the Neighbours Room and the frequent use of this room led to a rather strange visit from an official from the Planning Department of Northampton Borough Council who told us we would need planning permission if we were offering the room to groups other than members of our Community. So we became a little more circumspect but did not diminish our outreach activities. Wise as serpents, harmless as …?

We spent a good deal of time trying to integrate all the children into this unusual lifestyle but this was not easy, partly because the age range varied from Rowan who was a baby, to Sarah who was soon leaving school, and partly because it was counter-cultural and this was embarrassing for some. *Why can't you be like other parents?*

As an example of sharing, *all Neighbours cars are insured for 'any other driver'* so that they can be more widely used. We continued to alternate the Thursday meetings between 'Mary' and 'Martha' evenings and Pam reported that all were happy with this arrangement. The Mary meetings are not recorded in the minutes but there is evidence that we talked about *the theology of* agapes and shared our individual spiritual journeys.

Simon continued to develop the garden with more trees and shrubs with sporadic help from the rest of us. It was inevitably a child-friendly area, boys' football competed with herbaceous borders.

Surprisingly, bearing in mind all this collective activity, the Common Fund fell into deficit as members did not always pay the agreed contribution needed to meet the expense of maintaining the garden and the Neighbours room, about £1,500 p.a. After much discussion we tried a weighted contribution scale, *a figure of net income divided by number of people in household. Use of facilities to be considered.* This seemed to work as *Roger reported that several interim contributions had been received and the Fund was in credit again.*

During the 1990s the TV soap opera called *Neighbours,* imported from Australia, was popular, and this caused some confusion among local people who wondered if it was us, feigning Australian accents. So we decided to change our name to *The Neighbours Community. Simon felt this would be a good idea and the rest of us agreed.*

At a community away-day at Turvey Abbey we discussed *the need to reflect on the denominational diversity of our worship* as there were Anglicans, Catholics, a former Baptist, and a Quaker involved on a daily basis, and *closed with a circle dance and prayers and singing in the Celtic tradition.* The ecumenical nature of the Community was always regarded as a strength rather than a weakness and reinforced the view that Christian unity is more likely to come 'from the bottom rather than from the top'. Of course, there is scope for hierarchical discussion and formal agreements, but the reality is happening at ground level in groups like The Neighbours Community.

The *Turvey Feedback* minute reads: *It was agreed to implement the theme of hospitality ... to welcome people in rather than going out. As all the families at present were committed to stay at The Neighbours for a period of time, it was thought that this was a period of stability contrasting with the past couple of years where the community had undergone constant change ... Pam mentioned the need to minute these days accurately.* This accurate minuting has enabled the present writer to recall the history and it is significant that, with one exception, all the members did stay for a further eight years until we laid down the community in 2007.

### Year 17, 2000

The rotas for 2000 show that we pursued vigorously the policy of hospitality with a wide range of day events including guest evenings, Creativity Days, *Agape* suppers, Clay and Pray, Quiet Days, Barbecues, Singing Sunday. Before or since there had never been so many 'invitation events' at the Community. Pam was in the forefront of this and she was missed in the summer when we agreed for her to respond to a request from the Columbanus community in Belfast for her to be temporary leader for two months.

Richard was also much in evidence with organising events for the eight Tickle/Appleby children and we were sharply reminded of the importance of listening to them when *Emily and Sarah joined the meeting to ask us to take down The Neighbours plaques which are outside the front doors of each of the five houses. They said these plaques caused them embarrassment.* We agreed to do this with the exception of the one on 144 (The Neighbours Room) which was considered to be a community house. Not of their choosing, the children were living in a counter-cultural environment unlike their school friends. (A few years later, when the children were a little older, we put the plaques up again, with their compliance.)

This episode led to a *Kids' Conference* when the adults invited them to say what they would like to happen – *Talk With Your Mouth Full* produced a long list of ideas which, if we had accepted them all, would have taken up all our energy and thousands of pounds of expenditure, including building a swimming pool and an extension at the back of the houses to link them more closely together. We never built a swimming pool but there were a number of concerns to which we did respond such as *seven baby guinea pigs needing homes* (Clare and Pam), more communal football (Chris) (Pam shuddered).

Joe complained that *the Tickles' front garden was messy and Simon agreed to tidy it up a bit.*

In association with NACCAN we organised another *Gathering of Communities – an informal day for Christian residential communities in the midlands area. News/prayer/food/ discussion /garden / crèche / singing.* The assembled group listed:

- We are rooted in the Christian faith and prayer.

- Our communities are often fragile and at risk. Survival depends on our willingness to change.

- Ecumenical relationships are important to us.

- We need and appreciate the active support of friends from outside our communities.

However, although there was a lot happening in Christian communities across the country, we considered that NACCAN *may be moving away from emphasis on residential communities,* and we withheld our subscription. Later we paid-up but expressed the view that NACCAN at present *had little to offer The Neighbours Community in our work of sustaining and developing an alternative lifestyle.* We hoped NACCAN would be more involved with residential communities because there was no other organisation which brought them together, but this was not the view of the NACCAN committee.

There were two away-days in 2000 at Turvey. At the second one in November, we invited Sister Lucy, one of the Turvey Sisters, *to be with us throughout, to listen and to comment as and when she chooses.* This was the beginning of a continuing link with Sister Lucy who joined us on numerous occasions over the following few years. We valued her friendship and spiritual experience and wisdom. In effect, she became our 'visitor' and in due course we invited her to be an Honorary Member, one of only two such invitations during the whole span of the Community.

Relationships with our neighbours in Ardington Road were often a little fragile and we received a sharply critical letter from someone about 20 doors away. Simon, our peace-maker, responded to it by replying: *I felt quite upset by it ... and I think that letters are not the best way to communicate ... I hope you will reply so that we can feel a little more friendly towards each other*. They met to discuss the problem and became friends. Alleluia.

### Year 18, 2001

There was no change of membership between 1999 and 2004 so these were relatively stable years during which the programme of invitation events continued unabated. There were numerous Quiet Days and Creativity Mornings.

One of the highlights of 2001 was a unique *Spirituality and Breadmaking weekend course* in March, led by Mother Catarina who was visiting UK from a monastery on the San Juan Islands where Susan and I had stayed when visiting our son, Peter, who lived in Seattle. This had taken months to organise and twenty people came, talking of their spiritual journeys and each making bread loaves, under Mother Cat's inspiring leadership. We reckoned that an hour after the start of the weekend she knew everybody's name and a day later she knew their life histories as well. '*An out-of-this-world experience*', said Marlies Thomason and '*One of the best things we have done*', said Susan.

Going as a group to another place helped us to put aside some of the activities of our home environment and find space to reflect, '*to be still and know*' that we are always in God's presence. Therefore we made it a discipline of the community that, despite the difficulty of finding a date that everyone could keep free, we would continue to have an occasional community 'away-day' or 'quiet day' as well as providing such days for others at Ardington Road, as part of our common task. On several occasions we went to Turvey Abbey and were joined by

Sister Lucy, and one occasion we went to the House of Prayer in Northampton, invited by Philip Munch, the resident hermit.

We also all went to Shining Cliff, a remote Youth Hostel in Derbyshire, for a weekend in August 2001 This was anything but a quiet occasion, and Richard enjoyed himself organising some wild 'chase games' in the woods. *The person who sustained an arm injury (Roger) was a victim of his own foolhardiness.*

Back at home, Sammy the cat died. He had come to the Neighbours with John and Jenny, ten years earlier, and was a well-established character. When we were unable to make a decision someone said 'Let's ask Sammy, he's sure to know'. Bet the pet. The ponderous recommendations of some professional 'life coaches' did not often mention this option for decision-making. Sammy *was buried near Pam's garage. We think he was 17 years old, and he will be missed.* (See Appendix C.)

During the early Neighbours years we had been sorely tested by some of the people to whom we offered a home and, later on, as some of the community children grew into teenagers, rowdy parties were also a problem, both for us and for other people living in Ardington Road. At least once we had to call the police and there was no chance that we would be lulled into thinking that community living was a heaven on earth. Matthew at 140 was the subject of frequent minutes and eventually he went to live in Nottingham with a friend. We gave him £100 and a sandwich toaster and *He was pleased with the leaving present.*

The calculations for the Common Fund contributions showed large disparities of income between the four households, one earned twice as much as the other three. The garden continued to be well-used and, after many discussions, we splashed out and bought a large mower to try to keep the grass under control.

Once again we tried a Community evening prayer during Lent, and realised the 'advantages' that a monastic house had where the monks did not go out of the monastery to work. They had no individual incomes and no question that regular daily prayer times, 'the office', had priority. We were constantly trying to balance work priorities, children's needs, with a discipline of prayer and often achieving little success. The Benedictine rule states '*the prayer is the work of the monastery*' and perhaps this is only possible by taking vows of celibacy, poverty and obedience. We were unable to claim any of these three virtues, as we had partners, money and much debate about decisions.

A TV production company proposed to make a series for Channel 4 about several different *households and their daily life and particularly how they react to the national news*. One member suggested this could be part of our Christian witness and, although one Neighbour's household *would not be prepared to be involved*, we agreed to *suggest that the producer come and talk to us about it*. However, on the phone he considered we were too unrepresentative to be relevant.

Neighbours' open tea on Sundays was a valuable occasion for some visitors but the mix of people was a problem. At least one regular attender was sleeping rough and did not have access to soap and water. Another, with mental health problems, brought a present of a box of chocolate, but said he did not choose to spend Sunday afternoons in the company of others with similar problems to himself. His comment reminded me of Groucho Marx, when invited to join a prestigious New York club for celebrities, said ' I don't want to be a member of a club that accepts people like me as members'.

### Year 19, 2002
Without taking any formal decisions, the members were all involved in hospitality, sharing the house and garden with others, and this became the accepted common task of the community. Our tables and chairs were at full stretch on Maundy Thursday with 18 people for an *agape* supper and 30 came to a House Concert in May with two visiting singers *in the Celtic tradition*. About 50 turned up for a '*Jubilee Barbecue*' in July in aid of the soup kitchen and Richard's catering skills ensured that they were well fed.

After much planning, we organised a two-day Enneagram event at Turvey to which eight people came. *All agreed that it was a beneficial happening and Sister Lucy was an excellent teacher.* We decided not to charge the full cost of this to the participants and met the difference by a levy among Community members.

The venue for a planned Turvey Day was changed at short notice to a home day because some of the children were ill. This pointed up our attempts to balance the needs of families within the community. Sister Lucy observed that *we are formed by our prayers* and such formation was often under discussion. A minute in January reads: *a vehement exchange of opinions took place* about the times of community worship. Despite the vehemence, or perhaps because of it, we had the choice of six different agape liturgies *some of which were evolved here and some came from Iona, NACCAN, etc.* This was a fruitful time for developing appropriate liturgies for house groups.

The 'temporary' loan account to enable Richard and Patricia to rent 140 from the other members continued into its fourth year while they continued their search for an affordable mortgage. Pam generously raised the possibility of bequeathing 148 to the community by means of a charitable trust, but the legal problems defeated us and we abandoned the attempt.

The NACCAN co-ordinating team announced that they were recommending that NACCAN be wound up. As founder members we received this decision with some sadness but accepted that the enthusiasm for residential communities seemed to be diminishing. For four years, from 1993 to 1997, I had been editor of the NACCAN magazine, *Christian Community*, and to maintain contact between the hundred or so NACCAN members, I offered to produce a quarterly newsletter. The Community supported this. We called it *Touching Place* and it ran for ten issues until 2006. I have kept a full set of these magazines, including writing by world-renowned leaders of Christian communities. They form an unique record and an archive which may be useful to researchers in due course.

The garden workers were congratulated on making a *Jubilee Garden* at the end of 144, including trellis plants, seats for quiet sitting and a circular space for bonfires. This area also attracted groups of young people who chilled-out there and sometimes made a lot of noise. Occasionally the wingding got out of hand and on 12 August we had to call the police to remove some drunken gate crashers who were being abusive and violent; *all present were deeply affected by the fracas on Monday night.*

### Year 20, 2003

Simon and I, with support from all the members, spent some months planning a Mental Health Workshop, under the auspices of The Neighbours, to bring together people with mental health conditions and doctors and pastors working in this field. We sent out 90 letters and the response was such that it would be too large an occasion for Ardington Road, so we booked the main hall at Abington Avenue United Reform Church and this proved to be a good venue. The speakers were David Smart, Simon (doctors), and Chris Goodley (Chaplain at St Crispin's Hospital). Sixty people came, so this was a major event for us. We recouped the cost by charging £10 per head and The Neighbours Mental Health Trust made a balancing grant of £174. *We thanked Roger for the enormous amount of work he put into the day and decided to spend our next Mary meeting drawing together thoughts from the day into some kind of document to send out to the people who came.*

Susan and I, and Simon wearing a grinning Tony Blair mask, took part in the huge STOP THE WAR demonstration and march in London on 15 February 2003, with over a million people on the streets. Unusually for the community, as there were a variety of political affiliations among the seven members, we united in opposing the Government plans for declaring war on Iraq. *After a vigorous debate and five minutes' silence, seven letters were written to MP's ... all seven of us signed a NO WAR/ NOT IN OUR NAME declaration in the Daily Mirror.* None of this prevented Blair from declaring war and my confidence in him and New Labour never recovered from this disastrous military adventure.

The programme for the year, under the title *The Neighbours Community – an ecumenical community of households in Northampton*, included ten Quiet Days at 148 and eight Taizé prayers on Sunday afternoons which followed on after the weekly 'open tea '.

In June we celebrated *20 years of The Neighbours Community* but an away-day at Turvey drew attention to some of the problems: *We have become aware of a polarisation within the community between members who have demanding jobs or responsibilities relating to children, and tend to be unavailable for activities of outreach, and those who are more available but are getting older and have limited energy. We feel the time is right to expand the community without in any way altering the conditions of membership.* When this was written we little thought that the Community would soon change as Simon told us on 17 July that he and Deborah had decided that he *should move-out of 142 as soon as he could arrange some other place to live. They both hoped it would be a place where the children could visit him as freely as possible.* This separation came as a surprise and a shattering blow to most of us although, with hindsight, we realised that the question of Simon's sexual orientation had been brewing for some years. He bought a house just up the road from the Neighbours and the children were able to visit freely. *Simon pointed out that the move to 130 (Ardington Road) was a 'necessity'* and we agreed that he should remain a member of the Community as long as he wished. He continued to come to meetings and take an active part in community events.

I was delegated to speak to Moyna about her future. We wanted *someone to live in the flat who could be an active member of the Community. She said she did not feel able to join in anymore and she has recently been thinking of possibly moving in with her mother. Roger told her there was no immediate hurry for her to leave.* Moyna moved to her parents' home near Leicester in December 2003 after nine years at 144, the longest tenure of any non-member resident. We are glad to keep in touch with her and follow her progress in her work at a special school in Kettering.

We had been in touch with Stephan Ball for some months and agreed for him to join the Community in September. Simon rented a room to him at 130 Ardington Road and when Moyna moved out of the flat we offered to rent it to him as he was not in a position to buy a house. Stephan was the last member to join and stayed for four years until the Community ended in 2007. As a mental health nurse he found work in a local independent hospital and then with the NHS. He is a Quaker of long-standing and surprised us by saying *that he would be interested in organising a Eucharist for the Neighbours and others.* Early in 2004 he visited New Zealand and the Eucharist took place after his return in June.

For some years our Thursday evenings had alternated between Mary Meetings (discussion, bible study, theology, prayer) with Martha Meetings ( planning, dates, problems, decisions). This pattern had produced an acceptable balance but times were changing and *Simon suggested it might be a good idea to have more Mary evenings and less Martha evenings.*

At a Turvey Day in November, there was *a brainstorming session* about membership and *we united round a note written by Deborah … We affirmed Pam in her role as programme co-ordinator … and thanked Sister Lucy for joining us for the day and the Brothers for providing space and an excellent lunch. In December Susan introduced the topic of our intercessions. We talked about praying for the problem but not the name. We also noted that we tend not to pray for ourselves. We decided to have a notice board in the Neighbours Room... Simon would write an introduction.*

*Year 21, 2004*

When she lived in Surrey, Pam had opened her house as a place of prayer and invited people to stay for a few days as a quiet place. When she came to 148 she felt called to continue this ministry and people came to stay in her spare room on this basis.

Pam also continued to organise regular Quiet Days and Creativity Days, both of which became features of the community's life at this time. John Evans, vicar of our local parish church, led a day about St Patrick, Philip Munch from the House of Prayer in the town, presided at a communion service with us and visitors and so did Brother John, Prior of the Monastery of Christ Our Saviour at Turvey where Sister Lucy again joined us. We ran a Bible Sharing group, *in the manner of Quakers*, during Lent and sixteen people came to an agape supper on Maundy Thursday. All these occasions were deliberately ecumenical and interdenominational and we saw this *unity in diversity* as a fundamental part of our ministry. At the end of the year it was noted that five events taking place *at The Neighbours Community this week … are interdenominational … It is very unlikely that similar events would have taken place 20 years ago or even 10 years ago*. Although we had many visitors staying in one or other of the houses during the year we did not return to offering accommodation to people with mental health issues as we had done in the 1980s.

Discussions at Thursday meetings covered a wide range. Stephan *asked for views about whether or not he should buy a car [due to the dodgy handwriting of the agenda and perhaps also due to the fact that the meeting had been going on a long time, there was some uncertainty about whether we were discussing a car or a cat. The general view was that Stephan would not be able to get to work on a cat.]*

Simon wrote a letter to all members in June saying that he was *not a Christian any more though 'I will always adhere to the basic Christian principles of love and siding with the poor'*, which he was certainly doing at his doctor's practice in the town centre, offering health care to drug addicts and other patients, work which other GP practices shied away from. He wrote, *I'm eternally grateful for everything the Neighbours has done for me, but considered that he must leave the Community and we agreed, sadly, to accept Simon's view that he should cease to be a member ... We shall try hard to maintain personal friendships and to offer what support we can.* He had been a member for ten years and was very influential during that time, but we realised that the break-up of his marriage with Deborah and his entry into a new relationship made his membership untenable.

Simon's leaving was a set-back. Full meetings became difficult to arrange and our morale was diminished. In his leaving letter he had suggested that *perhaps ... you need to consider scaling down your activities somewhat! ... community meetings need to avoid being as 'business and news' orientated as they have recently become – they have lost their edge a little and are not challenging enough in terms of exploration and honesty ... for me.* Some months later, Stephan, as the newest member, *felt that the Community was in a state of transition* but there is no record of clarity about where the transition was leading. With the benefit of hindsight, perhaps this was a turning point.

The cost of producing the newsletter, *Touching Place* (Luke 6:19) was well within budget after four issues and, paradoxically, the Community finances were in good order in 2004. After discussing the annual accounts, we decided to distribute £400 back to Members. This had never happened before.

### Year 22, 2005

After six years with no change of membership, in 2004 we had lost Simon and gained Stephan so, at the beginning of 2005 the members were Deborah, Susan, Roger, Richard, Patricia, Pam, and Stephan.

In January we had an away-day at the House of Prayer attached to St Michael's Church and another at Turvey in April, led by Sister Lucy, *centred on the process of decision-making using Myers Briggs Type Indicator (MBTI) as a guide. Sister Lucy pointed out how the different preferences might affect our way of looking at problems.*

We must have accepted Simon's comment about too many 'business' meetings as henceforward we had two Mary meetings for every Martha one. The Mary evenings were not minuted so no record remains. The Martha meetings were dominated in 2005 by an unhappy and long-drawn out breakdown in relationships between two Community Members. They were asked to seek mediation help with Sister Lucy at Turvey but at the year end, the problem was not resolved and they were hardly able to be in the same room together. Not surprisingly, this failure affected all of us and I was ashamed that we seemed unable to repair the breakdown.

We tried optional evening prayers again in Lent. *Roger went a couple of times but otherwise no one remembered!*

The monthly house eucharist was better attended, sometimes presided over by one of us and sometimes by invited visitors such as Michael Jackson (Methodist) and Brother John (Roman Catholic). There was a general view that agapes would be more appropriate for these interdenominational occasions, but providing the food was an issue. Despite the problems I think we were making a valuable contribution to inter-communion on these informal evenings and they reinforced my view that progress towards Christian unity is just as likely to come from 'the bottom up' as from 'the top down'.

We noted a TV discussion between Melvyn Bragg and Archbishop Rowan Williams who said that many small communities are springing up in great variety and it was vital to keep good communications between the body of the Church and to put energy and support into these communities, many of which are 'on the edge'.

As always, we struggled to keep our large garden under control. *The lawn is still a great cause for concern. It is bare and waterlogged* .... In April, *football and games will be barred* to give the re-seeded areas a chance to take root. It was in reasonable shape for a Summer Gathering in August when thirty people from four different communities took part and nearly 100 came to the Soup Kitchen barbecue. However, by October *the garden is getting rather tangled up* and we discussed reducing some of the numerous trees.

The Common Fund, administered by Deborah who held the Nationwide Building Society passbook, and myself, the keeper of the tin in the cellar, recorded annual expenditure of about £2,000 for the year, paid for by contributions of £20 per month from members together with rent for the common areas.

### Year 23, 2006

Our discussions about eucharist and agape continued and our friend Michael Jackson wrote a helpful letter, noting the advantages in flexibility that intentional communities had over established denominations but warning us that *conflict between members of a large church can be accommodated in a way that is not possible in a small community*. A very relevant comment for us at that juncture. Michael gave his opinion that *a Christian community is defined by its worship*, and discussion clarified that we were not united round the liturgy of the Eucharist and would therefore lay it down for the time being. On the other hand, prayers in the style of Taizé and the agape evenings *seem to grow out of the life of the community, and as shared meals are a very meaningful part of our shared commitment to one another, continuing and developing this type of event seems a better way forward*. We spent £60 from the Common Fund on an updated set of Taizé songbooks.

We asked Lee Hodgson-King to visit and make some suggestions about the tangled garden and she recommended we make *five areas for meditation*. First however we had to do something about the two eucalyptus trees which we had planted some twenty years previously and had grown to over 15 metres and dominated the back area of the garden. This in turn led to an animated discussion about felling several other trees and a difference of opinion between the 'let it all grow naturally' faction and the 'cut it down before it engulfs us' group. A questionnaire led to a painful decision to fell six trees (two hollies, fir, peach, balsam poplar, vine maple) and retain five (two firs, two sumacs and a wild cherry).

Richard was designated *feller-in-the-sky and the rest of us would be the ground-force with ropes etc*. We forbade him to climb the two eucalyptuses and paid £400 to have them professionally 'topped' and reduced to 10 metres.

In June 2006 we celebrated the anniversary of the community and noted that continuity was uncertain. We took part in a day organised by The Well at Willen, a re-invigorated residential community which had previously been a monastic house. I was approaching eighty and decided to hand on the production of *Touching Place* to Peter Barnett who had recently moved from the Pilsdon community in Dorset to initiate a new community in Kent called Pilsdon at Malling. The buildings at Malling had been a monastic house and so both these new lay communities had their roots in vowed monastic orders which were no longer attracting people willing to take life vows.

The rift between two Members continued to dominate the Martha meetings and there are seven minutes about it, over a period of eight months. We agreed to pay the expenses of Richard Turnbull, a trained mediator, to travel from Nottingham in May, to talk to them both. Sister Lucy wrote a detailed comment after a Turvey away-day in July. Thereafter there seems to have been an 'uneasy truce'.

The issue was overtaken by a discussion in November 2006, again at Turvey. Deborah, who had been at The Neighbours for twelve years, longer than anyone else except Susan and me, wrote a comprehensive minute: *Susan felt that she no longer has the energy to complete practical tasks that she wants to, and wants to direct her energy towards her concern for the spirituality of ageing ... Deborah felt that recent changes in her life since she and Simon had separated had brought her to a point where she wanted to live in a more independent way.*

I was also ready for a change of lifestyle so the three of us gave notice to leave and start the one year process of finding new members to join the community and buy the three middle houses, 142/144/146. If none could be found then we might have to sell on the open market to enable the leavers to buy elsewhere. This would effectively end the Community as the two remaining houses 140 and 148 would be too far apart to function as at present. Sister Lucy added a reflection, referring to Susan and me as *the foundation stones* of the community, because we had been there since the beginning in 1984.

The four people remaining, Richard, Patricia, Pam and Stephan, *need to sort out how they come to decisions, otherwise the Community will not be able to move forward.*

Decisions could not easily be made until we had found new people to join and replace the three leavers, and we set about this task by circulating a note, *Opportunity To Join A Community.* We also published a piece in the local inter-church newsletter, LOGOS, which included the following: *One of the members remarks that living in The Neighbours Community is 'a roller coaster ride. Sometimes I feel we are knocking on the door of the Kingdom whereas at other times I ask what on earth am I doing here and is it different from where I was before?'*

The *Group of Five* (GOF) which had been the somewhat reluctant owners of 140 for eight years since the Appleby family had arrived in 1998, continued to press Richard and Patricia to negotiate a mortgage and buy the house. They were prepared to sell it to Richard and Patricia for £120,000 whereas the market price was in the region of £180,000, but many months would ensue before this sale could be completed.

*Year 24, 2007*

In response to our *Moving On* notice a number of people showed interest in joining the Community but none had committed themselves and in January we decided to approach other communities with a view to some kind of joint enterprise. A lovely wacky couple came from Cheltenham to have a look at us and we also discussed with a group from Milton Keynes. We even had a response from China!

In the meantime *the continuing group will have a meeting separate from Thursday evening, to decide how best to proceed.* They organised *A Day of Discernment* in June starting with a time of prayer followed by wide-ranging discussion One of the communities represented was Lee Abbey in Devon, a well-established Christian community considering an outreach house in the midlands area and interested in the possibility of joining-up with the continuing group. Over the summer months, several of their trustees and members visited us and *were enthusiastic to move the project forward.* In July our local vicar, David Wiseman, welcomed this initiative. *As well as parish life based on Christ Church, it would be a strength to have local examples of different ways of living the Christian life, such as community living.* One of the Lee Abbey trustees spent a day with us and *expressed a hope that a merger between Lee Abbey and The Neighbours Community would go ahead but also expressed some reservations.* He said it was a major financial decision for the Lee Abbey Council and we realised that it was also a theological decision because the focus of Lee Abbey had always been mission and personal salvation whereas the concerns of The Neighbours had been directed more towards Christian unity and the social gospel.

The chairman of their Households' Committee had a couple in mind as potential leaders of this project but in September he wrote to say they were no longer available: *most disappointingly for us, they have recently accepted another post.* So Lee Abbey had decided that they *are unable to proceed any further with the possibility of a purchase in Northampton. It is with very great regret that we reached that decision and I know it will be a great disappointment to you (Roger) and particularly to Pam, Richard and Pat, and Stephan. This was indeed a disappointment to all of us.* He also mentioned that they had *considerable demands including (but not only) financial, some of which have become apparent since we started our conversations in the Spring.*

Since November 2006 I had put a great deal of work into the search for a way forward, and so had the continuing group but the year's notice was now imminent. We met on 4 October at the specialist care centre where Pam was recovering from an injury to her neck and agreed the following minute:

*We have been seeking a buyer for the three centre houses, 142/144/146, to take forward The Neighbours Community as an ecumenical Christian community of households. The Lee Abbey Movement informed us on 7 September that they had decided not to proceed. It is unlikely that any other prospective buyer will come forward before the one-year notice expires, on 15 November. It was therefore AGREED that Deborah, Susan and Roger should proceed to put 142/144/146 on the market when they choose.*

I wrote a *Notice of Closure* to inform the many people with whom we were in touch:

*The members of The Neighbours Community have decided to draw the Community to a close on 2 December 2007 after nearly 24 years in Ardington Road. We give thanks for the friendships made, hospitality received and given, hopes and fears shared. As we go our various ways we say to all concerned, as we have said every day here at morning prayers, 'The Grace of our Lord Jesus Christ, and the love of God, and the fellowship of the Holy Spirit be with us all evermore'*

*Deborah and family, Pam, Patricia and Richard and family, Roger and Susan and Stephan.*

Each of us wrote down our feelings for a final discussion at Turvey Monastery on 31 October 2007, a unique record:

–We have many good and positive memories to take with us and to me this feels the right time to draw things to a close.

–We will remain always brothers and sisters in Christ whatever change occurs. Thank you to all the Neighbours for understanding and support over the years. It will never be forgotten.

–I feel that the time has come to allow Roger, Susan and Deborah to move their lives on and make a new start.

–The Neighbours has stood for ... an alternative to living in individual boxes, with an accessible pattern of worship ... For me the greatest sadness will be the destruction of the garden for, however divisive it has been latterly, we have created an amazing open space ... no more 'praying presence' each morning – that will be a real loss. We should go out with a shout not a whimper. We know that we have often not done what we set out to do but, for others, it has stood for something positive.

–We give thanks for blessings received, a time of grace, a different way to try to live out the Gospel over 23 years.

–It seems there are signs that The Neighbours Community is coming to the end of its life. This does not preclude some other form developing at a future date, but that is in God's hands.

At Turvey we sang our favourite Taizé chants and spent the morning *talking about our memories and experiences*. In the afternoon Pam led a session on *Changing Horizons, possibly looking towards the middle distance or the far horizon*. Sister Lucy talked about the 'neutral zone' where endings and beginnings *overlap.* Sister Lucy had been a valued friend and mentor for several years and we invited her to become an Honorary Member of the Community, for its final few weeks. *She was pleased to accept.*

Deborah closed the community bank account, I emptied the tin in the cellar and we 'divvied up' the balances.

The final members meeting was on Thursday 29 November:

*Deborah brought sherry and we nibbled stuffed olives. In silence we passed the bread and wine of the agape liturgy to each other. Susan had cooked roast vegetables, Greek style, and others had added lots of vegetables. Pam brought raspberry meringue. A truly contributory final supper together.*

*Deborah is dealing with stuff belonging to the community, including furniture, motor mower, worship books and crosses, (leaking) tea urn, teapots, an extending ladder.*

*Pam had counted 67 Creative Mornings in the Visitors Book and a number of Quiet Days. Richard recollected 9 barbecues, also 'murder mysteries' and carol singing. Roger had attended the last meeting here of The Order of St Luke and reported their thanks for hospitality over nearly 20 years and perhaps 1000 meetings.*

On the closing day, Advent Sunday, 2 December, *We invite all friends to come to tea and thanksgiving … there will be the usual Taizé prayer at 5.30pm. We look forward to seeing you.*

Mirroring the last line of T.S. Eliot's Journey of the Magi, 'We *returned to our places, these Kingdoms, but no longer at ease here in the old dispensation*', the last minute in the last book reads:

*We dispersed quietly back to our own places.*

## SUMMARY AND CRITIQUE

The Neighbours was a residential Christian community in five adjoining terraced houses in a suburban road in Northampton, UK. It started in June 1984 and ended in December 2007, a period of twenty-three-and-half years, long enough to experience what works and what does not work but short enough to avoid becoming encrusted with practices which have become irrelevant.

During the lifetime of the Community over fifty people lived at 140-148 Ardington Road at one time or another. The history of the Community is contained in considerable detail in thirteen Minute Books recording the weekly meetings, a total of about 3000 minutes and numerous supporting papers. It is rare to have such a detailed record of a counter-cultural project of this kind.

The purpose of the Community was:

*To develop a community life which enables us to explore and share our faith and care for others according to the Gospel.*

To what extent did we accomplish this purpose?

### Membership

Although we did not take any formal vows the understanding was that the decision-making Members of the Community were those who owned and lived in any of the five houses. We asked new Members to stay for a minimum of two years and, in the event, the shortest stay was four years. If we no longer wished to be Members of the Community we should give a year's notice and find a new Member to buy the house. We made one exception to the house ownership concept during the final years of the project when one Member was renting the flat in 144.

The benefit of this member/house owner pattern was stability and continuity because people who had bought a house were less likely to move on than those who were renting. There was

a total of fifteen Members and only four house sales during the
23 years. Most residential communities, both Christian and
secular, are based on renting rather than buying the property
and had much higher rates of membership turnover during these
years. The Directories published by the National Association of
Christian Communities and Networks (NACCAN) show that
numerous communities had a significantly shorter lifespan
than The Neighbours.

### Prayer and worship

In the sixth century that practical man, St. Benedict, declared
that the prayer is the priority 'work' of the monastery and it
could be said that prayer is the defining factor of every Christian
community. The corporate prayer life of The Neighbours varied
over the life of the Community and we were at our best when
the prayer was most accepted and prioritised by Members. It
became an unwritten rule that part of being a Member was
to lead morning prayers on a rota basis and the comments of
the latter Members in 2007 indicate the importance of this
daily discipline. The fact that Members were active in several
different denominational churches, Anglican, Roman Catholic,
Quaker, Methodist, did not present any visible problems for
morning prayers or other liturgies. There was a unity among us,
sometimes an impatient unity as we were confronted with the
dogged inflexibility of some local congregations.

The form of morning prayers varied but the basis was nearly
always included a bible reading and a time of silence, perhaps
five or ten minutes rather than the much shorter silences
experienced in most church services. Evening prayers were
tried on a few occasions but never became an integral part of
the life of the Community, nor did Eucharistic liturgies with the
notable exception of agapes, the breaking of bread and drinking
of wine as part of a meal together. There were years when we
had a monthly agape supper, often with visitors present, and
the Community records include a file of interdenominational

agape liturgies, prepared by community members. It is relevant to note that in each of the three descriptions of Jesus' institution of the symbolic bread and wine ceremony (Matthew 26:26-29; Mark 14: 22-25; Luke 22:14-20) it was part of a meal together, an agape rather than a stand-alone Eucharistic occasion such as a church service. So we regarded our adopted practice as being entirely Gospel-based.

Worship in the style of the Taizé Community in France was also a lasting format and the chants became well known to most of us. During the lifetime of The Neighbours Taizé worship, with its emphasis on repetitive singing of simple chants and prolonged periods of silence, became widespread in UK and we were glad to be part of this ecumenical liturgical movement. Like some of the well-known hymns, chants such as *Jesus Remember Me* and *Wait for the Lord* are now sung in many churches and Christian gatherings.

We also developed Bible sharing groups from time to time, basing them on a method developed by Quakers over many years. At The Neighbours some of us recollected Bible study as little more than being told what to believe by a priest or Sunday School teacher. Bible sharing is different; it starts from the conviction that God is present in each one of us and therefore each of us has some of the truth within us. A passage is read aloud from several different translations and then, in silence, each person writes down a response to five questions; What is the authors main point? Is this passage true to my experience? What problems do I have with this passage? What new light do I find in reading this passage to-day? What are the implications of this passage for my life? Each person then reads out his/her response or may choose to 'pass'. There may be brief requests for clarity but, at this stage, there is no discussion; our contributions are of equal value whether we are scholars or believers of long-standing or recent Christians or agnostics. A comment which may seem trivial to one person may be an important new insight to another. When all five questions have been answered there is then, but not till then, a time of general discussion. The study, which should not take more than an hour, may end with a prayer or period of silence. We found that this sharing approach was often appropriate for Community members.

We deliberately avoided becoming an alternative Sunday congregation but hopefully added to the concept of a wider inclusive church. As a friend said, *The Neighbours is the only congregation in town which meets every day except Sunday*. Amongst the handful of members who moved on from the Community, it is significant that two, Richard Hall (Methodist) and Jenny Parkin (Anglican) left to train for the ordained ministry. In addition, Michael Jones was a Reader in the Anglican church for many years and Richard Appleby, at the time of writing (2014) is the local convenor of Teams of Our Lady, the Roman Catholic organisation for married couples. Other members were and still are active in several congregations. Susan has led many Quaker groups and I have been happy to be asked to lead Taizé prayers in half a dozen different places.

The spiritual journey of each of us was always on the agenda and the development of this worship, morning prayers, agape, Taizé, demonstrated that it is possible and practicable for a very ordinary group of lay Christians to adopt a pattern of prayer, less rigorous than a monastery, but almost certainly more disciplined than any of us would achieve when living in a separate house rather than a community. Hundreds of Minutes and the comments of Members at away-days and the closing meeting in 2007 bear witness to this and, if there had been no other outcome, this alone might be regarded as justifying the existence of The Neighbours.

### Governance
Like knitting, so in a community, if it is too loosely tied together it tends to unravel and come to an end. If it is too tightly tied, it

becomes uncomfortable and unduly constrained. The decision-making structure of The Neighbours Community was the meeting of Members every week and the thirteen volumes of minutes are a record of hundreds of such meetings. We never appointed a chairman, secretary or treasurer but often allocated specific roles to individuals such as lead-gardener or keeper of the common fund. Each member chaired the meeting in turn and was responsible for writing up the minutes; some took to this easily, others found it a burden. Trawling through the minute books for this writing it seems that this simple low-key structure served us well although it was sometimes difficult to maintain a balance; meetings too long are tedious and unfruitful, meetings too short make it difficult for each to have their say. It seems that we hardly ever took a vote but waited for a consensus to emerge.

From the recorded comments over twenty years I detect two 'golden rules' for community members. Firstly, take issues to the meeting and do not make decisions unilaterally even if the right course seems obvious. Secondly, talk to others individually but only say what you are prepared to repeat to the assembled meeting. It also seems that those who said least at meetings sometimes made the most significant contribution. Those from congregations with a tradition of silence or tacit obedience sometimes had the most to say when the governance structure permitted them to speak. I believe Quakers are aware of this irony.

The weekly meeting sometimes became an unwelcome chore. Why spend time talking about community business when we could be drinking coffee or playing football? The early attempts to make signed formal Agreements about the selling of Community houses turned out to be a step too far. However, in times of difficulty, the acceptance of the weekly meeting carried us through and the Community would have ended much sooner if we had not had some such formal procedure for exchanging views and making decisions. The history of other contemporaneous communities seems to bear this out; those with little or no structure often failed to survive; those with carefully thought out governance tended to survive. The Benedictine Order is a classic case in point.

### The five houses

The concept of linked houses in a terrace worked well. Each household had its own space, but was much more closely connected than separate houses, however close to each other. The three initial houses, 142-146, had inter-connecting doors on both floors so that, for example, bedrooms could be added or subtracted from each household as the number of residents changed, young people leaving home or residents needing support from community members. There were many such changes. Patrick was proud of the fact that he had lived in each of the five houses at one time or another. The shared back garden without fences was also a linking factor as people could easily come and go to any of the houses without going out of the front door.

### House ownership

The member/house ownership policy was a considerable restraint and commitment for those considering joining but it did enable Members to stay on 'the housing ladder'. The Community years were a time of escalating house prices and the three initial houses which we bought for around £20,000 each in 1983 were selling for over £200,000 by 2007. If we had sold our house in 1983 to join a renting community we would have found it financially impossible to buy a house again in 2007. This is one reason why there are so few communities of families. Single people, not yet owning property, are better placed to join a religious order or rent a space in a corporately owned community house but most couples, particularly those with dependent children, would find this a much larger sacrifice and few of the households which comprised The Neighbours

Community would have joined on a renting basis. It is easy to say that such considerations were unworthy of those who were committed to Gospel values and perhaps we should have been willing to abandon house ownership and leave the outcome in God's hands but that would have eliminated most of us more hesitant Christians, unable to give up all such material concerns. We were trying to find a community lifestyle that 'could happen in any street'. However, our failure to find new members in 2007, which led to the closure of the Community, is evidence that our ownership arrangement was not going to be the pattern for many new Christian communities of households at present.

Perhaps we had departed too far from the open market to attract new members but such is the fate of pioneers. I was reminded of Jack Bellerby's plans for the original Neighbours in the 1930s. (See Appendix A). He wanted members to live on the average wage of the day, about 30 shillings per week, and put the balance of their earnings into a common fund to be used for projects to improve society. In the event, few of his friends were prepared to do this and the scheme was abandoned after a few years. So, fifty years later, we foundered on a different but equally resistant materialistic rock.

### A Common Task is Essential
The discipline of corporate prayers was an on-going commitment and we were, of course, supporting each other in living a somewhat counter-cultural lifestyle but the history indicates that, in addition, a common 'outside' task was essential to hold the community together. There were two phases.

Phase 1. 1984-1994 during which we offered supportive accommodation to a number of young people with mental disorders. Because there are two large psychiatric hospitals in Northampton, the problems of after-care are of more significance than in other towns of similar size, and we were only touching a small part of the need. We made no claim to professional medical knowledge of psychiatry and such expertise was not necessary for most of those who came within our orbit. What they asked for, usually after a spell in hospital, was some understanding of their need to integrate back into life in the wider community and some patience when their behaviour was unusual or socially unacceptable. In our many discussions about the way to respond, and in our prayers, we attempted to follow Jesus' teaching to stand alongside those in greatest need and when he mentioned the happiness of 'the poor in spirit' (Matthew 5:3), perhaps he had in mind some of the people with mental disorders who feature in the Gospels? (Matthew 8: 28-32)

We found this to be a demanding task and there were some disappointments but we know now, as we are still in touch with several, that living at The Neighbours Community helped a number of needy people to find a less dependent and more rewarding lifestyle.

Phase 2. 1994-2007 during which we adopted non-residential hospitality as our common task. During this time we organised a programme of corporate worship and day events. The Neighbours Room and the garden were widely used by all kinds of groups. Members' varied experience of community living and informal worship were passed on to many people, especially those on the fringes of Christian congregations.

The Community was at its weakest when an agreed task came to an end, usually because of a change of membership, and at its strongest when the outside task was freely accepted by all the current members. The common task was the glue that held the Community together and without it I doubt if The Neighbours would have survived as a Christian community for nearly a quarter of a century.

### Garden

In a crowded suburban area the norm was a narrow strip of garden behind each house, but by knocking down four fences we were able to make a large rectangular space with room for about twenty trees and plenty of grass. The Community was fortunate in having some keen gardeners among the Members and the garden was a wonderful facility for all manner of events, including discussion days, community breakfasts during the summer months, quiet days, barbecues. There was room for a large marquee on the lawn and there were several wedding receptions and numerous family parties.

We heard from a very elderly resident in Ardington Road that when the houses were built in the 1930s, it was normal practice to keep a pig at the bottom of the garden. We discussed this possibility but rejected it as a step too far. At one time we looked after chickens for a friend and there were several dogs, cats and numerous small animals which lived out their short lives in comparative comfort. Fish were in the pond and eaten by a heron from time to time, and a small turtle lived at 142 for several years.

There were times when the upkeep of the garden appeared to be a burden but there is no doubt that it was a wonderful asset for the life of the community and our outreach to others.

### Some conclusions

People living up and down the road up during the early days of The Neighbours Community tended to view us with suspicion and disfavour because we used the houses and gardens in a different way. We associated with people recovering from mental illness and this was seen to be 'bad for the neighbourhood' and might depress house prices in the road. We tried to be helpful neighbours and made numerous friends but also had a few arguments.

The best that can be said about achieving our purpose, *'according to the Gospel'*, is that we did share our faith and developed a discipline of prayer and worship, beyond anything we could have done alone. The Community also made a significant contribution towards caring for people with mental disorders which could not have been achieved by a single household. We were also able to offer much more hospitality to individuals and groups.

A significant weakness was the procedure we adopted for buying and selling the houses by private sale rather than the conventional arms-length market price. This caused uncertainty about how those who moved-on would re-enter the housing market and was a contributory factor in the closure of the Community in 2007, because new members could not be found. Benedict knew better; his communities have survived and contributed for 1500 years!

Susan and I knew in 1983 that we were entering into an uncertain but long-term commitment to an unusual lifestyle and we have no regrets except the failure to find other people to replace us when we moved on in 2007. We remain in touch with all the Members who were such an important part of our lives and I am sometimes surprised and pleased that those who were children during the Community years have such cheerful and positive memories of people, house and garden.

This writing has been personal and subjective as part of my life story but there remain the thirteen Minute Books in a large box and I hope that someone may one day use them to write a more objective account that may be useful to people considering Christian community living.

## CHAPTER 4

# Some examples of small residential Christian communities

Within the definition on p.16, here are some examples of small residential Christian communities 'under one roof' in the UK in 2014.

**Carrs Lane Lived Community** is a small ecumenical residential community in Birmingham. The community flat accommodates five people. The community is committed to a routine of daily prayer, living and eating together, shared financial responsibility, a spirit of hospitality and voluntary service.
**www.carrslanelivedcommunity.org.uk**

**The Quaker Community** at Bamford, near Sheffield, started in 1988 and has passed through several transformations. It occupies a substantial house that was formerly the offices of the local water board and has 10 acres of land part of which is an organic garden. Residents are Members or Attenders of the Religious Society of Friends (Quakers) and meet for worship morning and evening. The community aims to be *'a radical witness in a competitive, individual and materialistic world'* and *'to give expression to Quaker testimonies'* by running courses and offering accommodation to visitors.
**www.quakercommunity.org.uk**

**Clapton Park URC Church Community House** provides low-cost accommodation and community living for Christians *who have made a commitment to live* in the Clapton area of east London. At June 2014 eight people live at this community house, some of them working with the URC church. The house was purchased by means of loans made by church members and others.
**www.63medianroad.blogspot.com.uk**

**Urban Expression**, which has roots in the Anabaptist tradition, is a *'very low-cost mission agency'* which *'recruits, equips and deploys'* groups in urban areas. It started in 1997 and now has 100 members, with groups in London, Wolverhampton and Manchester. Each group is self-financing and some live in community, sharing resources and adopting a simple lifestyle.
**www.urbanexpression.org.uk**

**The Iona Community**, mentioned earlier, is widely dispersed with over 200 Members and several thousand Associate Members and Friends, living all over UK and elsewhere in the world. Some are ministers and others are lay people. The residential centres on the island of Iona are run by a group of about 20 people, termed the Resident Staff Group, who are a residential community as they live under one roof and gather daily for prayer and to eat together. The leader of this group, termed Warden, is a Member of the Iona Community and the group usually includes some Associate Members as well as others who are not formally linked to the Iona Community on a long-term basis but are expected to conform to the practice of the resident group.
**www.iona.org.uk**

**The Chemin Neuf Community**, *'A Catholic community with an ecumenical vocation'*, includes men and women, married and single, from various denominations, united by their faith

in Jesus Christ. Traditional vowed monastic communities are receiving few vocations and a number have closed or joined with others. This releases premises, and a former priory in Sussex is now a Chemin Neuf community of people from all walks of life They also have a presence in Liverpool, where an Anglican priest is a member, and in London. In February 2014, '*in a joyful ceremony ...*' Archbishop Justin Welby welcomed four members of Chemin Neuf from three different denominations, to live at Lambeth Palace and share in a daily life of prayer, as a '*radical and exciting step for Christian unity*'. Not only for Christian unity but also for the development of new lay communities, Chemin Neuf's policy of making use of monastic buildings, no longer required by nuns or monks, is also a radical and exciting step.
**www.cheminneuf.org.uk**

**The Well at Willen** is a faith-based community of families, couples and single people who '*are attempting to live a shared expression of life through values of spirituality, hospitality, inclusivity, peace and justice and sustainability*'. Founded in 1997, The Well occupies a large house in Milton Keynes, with a library, meeting rooms and three acres of land. The community is '*Christian-based but welcomes people from different faith traditions and none*'. Members, currently seven adults, sign up to a mission statement and come together daily for meals and times of prayer.
**www.wellatwillen.org.uk**

**L'Arche** communities, mentioned earlier, founded by Jean Vanier in 1964, are all over the world. They define their identity as '*people with and without intellectual disabilities who share life together*'. L'Arche people live alongside each other under one roof and most such groups are small enough for all the community members to sit round one table. Each house is thus a small residential Christian community.
**www.larche.org.uk**

**Servants to Asia's Urban Poor**, commonly known simply as Servants, is a network of Christian communities living and working in urban areas of Asia and elsewhere in the world, participating with the poor '*to bring hope and justice through Jesus Christ*'. There has been a Servants team in Southall, west London, since 2008.

**www.servantsasia.org**

**The Sheldon Community**, the home of the Society of Martha and Mary, has been evolving slowly and steadily since 1991 on a beautiful 45 acre site in Devon. The five members of the Community all live on site and share a simple pattern of life together, caring for guests and offering time-out for retreats. They pray together twice a day. '*We're very serious about God but don't shout about it all the time*'. Their themes are '*gentleness, efficiency, small miracles and enjoying a good party*'.

**www.sheldon.uk.com**

**Ashram Community**, based in Sheffield since 1967, brings together several projects including a multi-faith chapel, library and shop in a relatively deprived inner-city area. There are several Community Houses each of which is a small residential Christian community seeking to live out '*a radical Jesus theology*'. Registered charity no. 1099164.

**www.ashram.org.uk**

**The Jesus Fellowship Church** is a large dispersed charismatic, christocentric organisation. It runs a substantial drop-in centre in Northampton including a cafe and facilities for disadvantaged people. Some church members live in community houses each of which is a small Christian community. I have been a passive supporter of the Jesus Centre, 'on the notepaper', since it opened in 2004.

**www.jesus.org.uk**

Here are two examples from other countries:

**Rutba House**, Durham, North Carolina, is an example of 'new monasticism' in USA where Bonhoeffer's phrase is more widely known than in UK. Linked to a Baptist congregation, Rutba House is a residential community founded by Jonathan and Leah Wilson-Hartgrove and others in 2003 with an over-riding concern to develop a *movement of radical reform based on God's love* (*New Monasticism*, J. Wilson-Hartgrove, Brazos, 2008). Members do not normally take vows nor wear habits but their lifestyle differs sharply from the way of life which has become the norm in USA. Rutba House and numerous other new monasticism communities in USA emphasize four values; prayer and contemplation, communal lifestyle, hospitality, practical engagement with the poor. Relocation/redistribution/reconciliation in Christ. In 2004 a seminal gathering of communities in USA suggested Twelve Marks of a New Monasticism (see Appendix E).

*New Monasticism.* J. Wilson-Hartgrove (Brazos 2008)

**Taizé Community**, Burgundy, France. Starting in the 1940's with a concern for Christian unity, thousands of young people from all over the world now visit Taizé for a week of prayer, singing, silence and discussion. With over 100 vowed Brothers, it is not a small community but, at any one time, some of the Brothers are living off-site as part of their work and witness. Wherever they are in the world they live and work in the very poorest areas and their houses in these places are small residential Christian communities. Their only extended sojourn in the UK was in Sheffield in 1958 when one Brother worked as a labourer in a steelworks and another, an experienced qualified psychologist, found employment as a porter at Sheffield Children's Hospital. **www.taize.fr**

And here are two examples of small vowed communities which, although they are marginally outside the scope of this book, were significant influences on The Neighbours Community. Their commitment to the Gospel is at a higher level than was ours:

**The Monastery of Christ Our Saviour**. At Turvey, near Bedford, a small group of vowed monks live a contemplative life under the Benedictine Rule, sharing daily worship with the nuns of the Priory of Our Lady of Peace on the same site. In 1980, their founder, Dom Edmund Jones, stated that it was his desire that they should look for *a serious life of prayer and the creation of a beautiful liturgy; a very simple lifestyle; a 'space' for silence; some hard work; and the constant search for Christian unity*. The Members of The Neighbours Community went to Turvey for many 'away-days' over a period of twenty years. Sister Lucy, from the Priory, was a valued accompanier and became an Honorary Member.

**www.turveymonks.co.uk    www.turveyabbey.org.uk**

**The Community of the Transfiguration** at Roslin near Edinburgh. When we lived in Sheffield we met Roland Walls and John Halsey. Both of them moved to Scotland and were the inaugural members of this unusual vowed community in 1965. Both were ordained Anglican priests. Roland, contemplative, joyfully irreverent theologian, prophetic teacher. John, contemplative, manual worker and shop steward. For almost 50 years, the Community has occupied a large 'tin hut' which had previously been a miner's reading room, together with an assortment of garden sheds, one of which is their chapel. Their vocation is to remain small and relatively unknown. Their concerns are hospitality, identification with the poor, a simple lifestyle. For years they had no phone and there is no website. Roland died in 2011 aged 93. The Community, with its wonderful counter-cultural features, is described by John Miller in *A Simple Life* (St. Andrew's Press 2014)

And lastly, a significant new community in the making:

**The Community of St Anselm**. A small interdenominational residential Christian community planned to start in 2015. Influenced by the Benedictine rule of life, Justin Welby, Archbishop of Canterbury, has announced plans for a group of young people to live in community at Lambeth Palace for a year. They will commit themselves to a monastic life of prayer, study and service and will be supported by the four members of Chemin Neuf who have been living at Lambeth since 2013. They will not necessarily continue in the monastic life at the end of the year, but the hope is that the experience will assist them in living the rest of their lives '*in deep communion with God*', perhaps working in industry or education. Archbishop Welby will be the abbot of the community.

## CHAPTER 5

# What is the future? Some reflections

I have noticed that when a candle is lit the small initial flame grows rapidly to a larger flame and then dies back to a steady medium flame which eventually burns out, Perhaps this is a parable for the kind of Christian communities under discussion, many of which light candles for prayers and meals. The community starts as a small enthusiastic counter-cultural group and, because of the enthusiasm and the vision of a Christocentric lifestyle, others are attracted, like moths to the candle flame, and the community grows. However, a limiting size is reached, governed by the amount of living space available or the needs of the common task, so the community levels out, reaches an appropriate size and continues as a stable group, maybe for just a few years or maybe for generations. In due course, circumstances change, perhaps the vision fades or the witness is diminished by differences of opinion or shortage of money or changes in social conditions. The community burns out, the flame is extinguished. In the case of The Neighbours Community this lifespan was 23 years; in the case of some Benedictine orders it is over 1500 years and counting.

Writing to his brother, Karl, in 1935 about the situation of the Church in Nazi Germany, Dietrich Bonhoeffer, the Protestant pastor who opposed Hitler and was executed by the Gestapo in 1944, says that renewal:

> *must surely come from a new kind of monasticism which will have only one thing in common with the old, a life lived without compromise according to the Sermon on the Mount in the following of Jesus. I believe the time has come to gather people together for this.*

(*The Life and Death of Dietrich Bonhoeffer*, M.Bosanquet, Hodder & Stoughton, 1968)

Some translations of this prophetic paragraph give 'banding together' rather than 'gather'. This is not to do with making music, though plenty of communities do make music, but is to lay stress on the cohesive nature of the kind of residential communities that Bonhoeffer had in mind, a stronger word than 'gather'. The residential community he formed in 1935 with young pastors in training at Finkenwalde started the day with common prayer, followed by breakfast, meditation and study. In the 80 years since then the courage of his Christian witness and the power of Bonhoeffer's writing have influenced many communities and some of his phrases such as 'new monasticism' and 'banding- together' have passed into the vocabulary.

With regard to what she calls '*the upside down world of God's reign*' Janey O'Shea writes:

> *In the topsy turvy world of the way of God as taught by Jesus, familiar categories turn upside down ... a woman who prefers intellectual discussion to housework is highly valued, the unemployed get a day's wage for a few hours' work ... a prostitute is held up as a good example to a religious leader ... the good seats at a state banquet go to the street people ...*

(Janey O'Shea, Backhouse Lecture, 1993)

These two quotations, sixty years apart, set the scene for anyone contemplating living in an intentional Christian community. Some 'familiar categories' may be turned upside down. That extraordinary man, Benedict, was concerned with vowed communities of monks but the Rule he initiated is relevant to all communities whether they are long established or new in the twenty-first century. Benedict wrote that the prayer of the monks was their primary 'work' and nothing should be allowed to stand in its way. If this primacy was abandoned then the monastery would eventually fold. Few lay communities today attempt to meet three times every day to pray together in the Benedictine pattern but a discipline of common prayer is essential and if it is lost, the community is lost with it.

In answer to the question *What are the factors encouraging the development of more small residential Christian communities to-day?*, a member of the Servants community in west London lists:

- We feel the hollowness of an individualistic lifestyle and consumerist culture and long for something richer and deeper.

- A realisation that to survive and thrive – individually, culturally and environmentally – we must rediscover our need for each other, and relearn how to share and work together.

- A sense that following Jesus to-day requires us to leave behind the trappings of empire and love of power, live simply and make room for those on the margins. We discover that we can't do that alone.

- Deep concern about poverty, inequality, and the environmental crisis affecting us all, and a desire to bring hope and healing or at least find a lifestyle that is more part of the solution than part of the problem.

- Disillusionment with traditional models of church and a search for something more holistic, authentic and grounded.

- A dissatisfaction with abstract theories and theologies and a longing for a lived spirituality that is practicable.

- A move of the Spirit, drawing on the example of others who have modelled this way.

- Alongside the idealism that draws some of us into community, there is often a relational factor that is equally important if we are to commit to and stay with a particular group of people, with all their wounds and limitations. It is something which equates to 'falling in love' - with a place, a people, a life – and brings with it a deep sense of call and belonging.

In answer to the question *What factors prevent the development of more small residential Christian communities?*, he suggests:

- Experience leads to the discovery that community life is hard at times!

- The prevailing cultures and lifestyle turn out to be hard to leave behind.

- Competing demands on time and energy as well as a reluctance to commit to anything long-term.

- High expectations of community combined with lack of experience of it can easily lead to discouragement.

## Economic considerations

In former times when the UK was a subsistence economy there is little evidence of intentional communities as we know them to-day because most people lived in villages where the tasks of providing shelter and growing food were shared and co-operation was taken for granted and essential to get the harvest in or the potatoes planted or the roof repaired. It was almost impossible for one person or one family to make an independent living. Only the king in his castle or a handful of nobles could afford to ignore their neighbours if they chose to do so.

This pattern disappeared as the UK became a trading nation but there was an interesting return to a measure of co-operation in my lifetime. World War II brought people together in unaccustomed ways. We were encouraged to accept evacuees from large cities, to protect public buildings by fire-watching, to grow food in the back garden ('Dig for Victory') or to join the Home Guard to defend the country in the event of invasion (as was immortalised by the TV series Dad's Army). In the immediate post-war years when food was still in short supply and the country exhausted by the six wartime years, this co-operative spirit remained and many small residential Christian communities resulted. However, as we became more wealthy towards the end of the twentieth century, we were able to survive and prosper in material terms, if we chose, by adopting a less co-operative and more individualistic lifestyle. The Conservative government's policy of an unregulated economy encouraged such individualism and enabled large companies to bring huge advertising pressure to bear on us to add to our possessions. The Englishman's home had indeed become his castle and every castle needs its own lawn mower and deep freeze as well as a car or two outside the walls. In the USA the percentage of the population living in suburban areas increased from 27% in 1950 to 37% in 1970 and a corresponding trend followed in the UK.

We favoured a square box of a house in a leafy suburb to get away from the congestion and crime in city slum areas and we wanted a place where thieves would not break in and steal from us, so we pulled up the drawbridge every night by locking the doors and putting the cat out. The mortgage is our moat and the burglar alarm our sentry on the ramparts. In consequence, the number of small residential Christian communities declined in the 1990's and 2010's and it took another generation to realise that in our concern for these commendable comforts, affluent privacy, we had ignored the problems of loneliness and lack of community.

Thus the state of the economy has a bearing on the development of intentional communities. An upturn nudges us towards a more secure 'castle' with a four metre security fence and a guard dog at the gate; a downturn inclines us to consider joining up with others to form a community. To take extreme examples, I see little evidence of residential communities in wealthy places like Monaco or Luxembourg.

In the UK even small variations in personal wealth are likely to influence the development of communities. The prevailing culture is primarily concerned with possessions whereas the Gospels repeatedly portray Jesus as living a simple uncluttered life and associating with all manner of people. It is his example that often moves us to be dissatisfied with the current models of Sunday church and to look for a significantly different lifestyle. Although there are hermits and individual saintly people who achieve this on their own, some realise that such counter-cultural practice is more likely to be achievable if we 'band-together' under one roof.

We want to bring hope and healing to the deprived and aspire to be part of the solution rather than part of the problem. We are aware of the huge inequality of our society in which, for example in London, a handful of billionaires live a stone's-throw away from areas of dire poverty and dependence on food banks. Perhaps it is remarkable that more stones do not get thrown over the high security fences that surround the rich.

Of course there is nothing new in these longings and historically we would be drawn towards the long-established monastic orders but we seem to be more fearful than our predecessors of abandoning our given circumstances. We hesitate to make life vows and thus it seems that vocations to traditional monasticism may be inversely linked to the standard of living, The richer we are the more difficult it is put aside the economic power that such riches brings. Jesus was well aware of this and spoke about it on several occasions, such as his debate with the rich man. (Luke 18:23). By his concern for the disadvantaged and his habit of associating with social outcasts such as tax collectors, he stepped right outside the conventions of his time. It is his example that often moves people to follow but we are hemmed-in by the social conventions of our time, the concern to be appreciated by those around us, to be successful at work, to be a 'domestic goddess' at home, to accumulate the possessions that advertisers thrust upon us. We are frightened of being humiliated by failure. We admire those few who take the huge step of joining a vowed community of monks or nuns but most of us do not feel called to the traditional monastic life and if we did feel called, we might not have the strength of mind to accept such a calling. Jean Vanier writes about the *'tyranny of normalisation'* by which he means the unquestioning acceptance of the prevailing culture, the tacit assumption that the consumerist lifestyle depicted by the popular press and soap operas are the only option.

When I was young my family had little money and Susan claims I was raised in 'genteel poverty'. Neither of my parents had ever been well-off and we children accepted our lifestyle with very little complaint; there was food on the table and a roof over our heads and it did not seem to bother me that many of our friends were more prosperous. Over the years our possessions and bank accounts seem to have accumulated and now I have to discipline myself from spending too much time on guarding the stuff, moving it from one place to another. I tell myself that it is to ensure that we do not become a financial burden to our children if we reach a stage when we need to live in a care home where the fees climb higher every year. As we gain prosperity we risk losing the ability to share and thus reject the community option because we feel the need to look after our pile of possessions. Perhaps this is one reason for the blossoming of communities in the 1970s and 1980s but not thereafter because of our increased prosperity; the 'love of money' tends to make us more isolated in our castle and less co-operative.

A harassed young farmer kept his goats in a field where there was plenty for them to eat and a good shed for shelter. The goats had no worries about their own comfort but, being goats, they wanted more freedom and were continually trying to escape. They looked for holes in the hedge or weak points in the fence and as quickly as the farmer repaired them, the goats found another outlet. 'You have to be aware, lad,' said his friend, an elderly retired farmer, 'you have many tasks around the farm but those goats have only one concern. Twenty four hours a day they are considering ways to get out. They have nothing else to think about. No wonder they can outwit you.' The goats were comfortable and 'wealthy' but instead of being content they used their affluent leisure to search for more 'freedom', thus making life more difficult for their owner. No wonder Jesus talked about camels and needles; sometimes our affluence is an impediment to the coming of the Kingdom.

In the early years of The Neighbours Community in the 1980s, there was widespread interest in community living demonstrated by several large gatherings of people living in community. At times we had a waiting list of people who might like to join us. But a generation later with a significant increase in the material standard of living, we failed to find replacements for two households moving on and the community came to an end in 2007. I note that half the communities we were in touch with in the 1980s no longer exist in 2014. Something had shifted. So the future for intentional communities depends partly on the state of the economy. The recession which followed the financial crash of 2008 has not sent many people scurrying to initiate residential communities but if we were faced with a much longer and deeper economic downturn we might expect renewed interest in community living as a natural extension of students sharing a rented house.

## Buildings

Single people who do not own a property can join a residential community such as a L'Arche house or the Resident Staff Group on Iona, perhaps receiving a modest allowance. They can move on in due course. However, anyone owning a house has a major decision to make to join a residential community and it takes a strong faith to step off the housing ladder at a time of escalating house prices.

Finding a suitable building is obviously a key factor in the inauguration of a new community. The group that eventually became The Neighbours Community spent over a year searching for one and we looked at half a dozen possible houses before finding one to buy (and it is my belief that we were led by the Spirit in eventually discovering three adjacent houses, all for sale at the same time). Some embryonic groups never become residential communities because they do not find a suitable building that they can afford to buy or rent.

One option is to venture into 'crowd-funding', made possible by the internet, whereby it is possible to raise loan money from among the vast and growing number of internet users, perhaps to buy a community house or to commission a purpose-built place. For example, a URC church in east London raised loans from the congregation and friends to buy a community house which is owned by a housing association. The percentage of the total value of the house was calculated for each lender so that when the house is sold (which they plan to do in three years' time) each gets the same percentage of the sale price. In this way, the lenders benefit from any increase in house prices which makes it an attractive proposition for people wanting their savings to be used in a beneficial way. Community members pay a rent to the housing association to cover the common expenses in the normal way and are not 'locked-in' by house ownership as was the case in The Neighbours Community. For more information on this procedure go to **www.63medianroad.blogspot.co.uk**

Another possibility is to adapt a pattern that has emerged for providing housing for older people. A development company constructs a purpose-built block of flats with some common facilities such as a meeting room, laundry room, guest accommodation, sells each flat to recoup the building cost but retains the freehold and manages the project to make an income. This may be a company intending to make a profit, or, alternatively, the freeholder may be a not-for-profit group with a shared concern. There is a growing number of such 'co-housing' projects most of which are not Christian communities as defined because the common link of the participating households does not include a common faith commitment. The common ground may be a shared ecological or social concern to create something together which any one household would be unlikely to be able to do on its own. Nevertheless, this organisational pattern could be used by a group of people called to create a Christian residential community.

A further option, which may become more frequently chosen henceforward, is to rent or buy premises that have been vacated by a religious order. Vocations to vowed orders have been decreasing for most of my lifetime and numerous monastic communities have sold or leased their redundant buildings, and in some cases have demolished them as unsuitable for any alternative use! Three of the examples of residential communities described above (Iona, Chemin Neuf, The Well) occupy former monastic buildings and organisations like Chemin Neuf, with close links to the Roman Catholic Church, have been able to secure the use of such buildings to initiate new intentional communities comprised of *people from all walks of life*. This indeed is Bonhoeffer's 'new monasticism' come to pass, arising phoenix-like from the old monasticism.

I know a Benedictine community of nuns which has not had a new Sister for nearly twenty years and this is probably not untypical of numerous other monastic houses. They have the financial resources to keep going due to endowments and the generosity of past and present benefactors, but in the longer run, no amount of money is sufficient if there are no new people to continue this particular form of religious life. So it is likely that more monastic buildings will be vacated and from the foregoing, it seems there are a number of ways in which small groups of Christians can find suitable premises to be a residential community. Hopefully this will lead to an increase in lay intentional communities over the years to come.

## Denominations

Traditional monasteries are nearly all specifically denominational, Roman Catholic, Anglican or Orthodox, but it is significant that most of the lay 'new monasticism' communities are interdenominational. Some were initiated on a denominational basis such as Iona (Church of Scotland) and Taizé ( Protestant/Reformed) and have moved to a more interdenominational membership during the past few decades. The Well at Willen, for example, grew out of an Anglican community but now *'welcomes people from different faith traditions'*. The Neighbours Community, starting in 1984, soon adopted an interdenominational stance and the fifteen members included Methodists, Anglicans, Roman Catholics and Quakers. One of the five houses was passed on to us by a lifelong Baptist.

These examples indicate that people concerned with residential communities tend to be ecumenical in outlook and accept that following Jesus in the light of the Gospels is more important than the denominational factors which sometimes keep us apart. Assuming this tendency continues, it widens the field for future communities. It will also affect liturgical development. It is significant that during the last few decades the theological teaching of Dietrich Bonhoeffer, the powerful prayers of George MacLeod of Iona and the repetitive chants of Taizé have all gone way beyond their denominational beginnings.

## Summary

When compared to an individual household the strengths of a small residential Christian community include:

- An agreed discipline of prayer, bible reading, (the 'work' of lay monasticism)

- Mutual encouragement for the journey of following Jesus ('better together')

- Ability to achieve an agreed task 'for others' ( action for poverty/disability/ healing/environment/food growing etc.)

- A witness for Christian unity (most communities are interdenominational)

- Economies in living expenses due to sharing of housing costs (rates, insurance, garden etc.)

- An answer to loneliness ( avoiding depression)

Weaknesses include:

- Irritation and stress caused by inability of members to avoid each other ('I need my own space')
- Financial risk of coming off the housing ladder in a time of rising house prices. ('Will we ever be able to buy our own place again?')

Opportunities include:

- Availability of redundant traditional monastic premises (e.g. Chemin Neuf, The Well, etc.)
- A measure of security in the event of recession descending into economic melt-down ('Our country is so deeply in debt that future economic catastrophe is inevitable'. 'Young people to-day are likely to be the first generation ever to experience a lower material standard of living than their parents')

Threats include:

- The 'tyranny of normalisation'. Despite the foregoing economic long-term expectation, our current affluence makes it hard to decide to adopt a simpler and counter-cultural lifestyle. ('Why can't you be like everyone else?')

I can think of no better way to end these reflections than to repeat Bonhoeffer's concern that there needs to be *a new kind of monasticism … a life lived without compromise according to the Sermon on the Mount in the following of Jesus. I believe the time has come to gather people together for this.* Bonhoeffer was a prophet as well as a martyr and perhaps the time is now coming for more people to gather together as small residential Christian communities.

# *Appendix A: Jack Bellerby*

### JACK BELLERBY - 'Contributive' Philosophy

Jack and Rosalind Bellerby were a wonderful couple of Oxford academics. Jack had been appointed Professor of Economics at Liverpool University in 1930 at the unusually early age of 33 but stood down few years later.

Jack was aware of the inequalities of UK society in the 1930s and, in a typical but very unusual move, he decided to put his principles into practice by living on the average wage of the time, two pounds per week for a single person, and giving away the balance of his professorial salary. He also stood as a Parliamentary candidate for the Labour Party in 1932.

He wrote extensively on economics and agriculture and set out his philosophy in *A Contributive Society* in 1931, including support for co-operatives. This brought us together in the 1970's when I was self-employed and we had many discussions about how to put some of his ideas into practice. For example, he considered that if enough people are willing to pay a little above the market price for food and this extra is returned to the producer in the developing world, then there will be a significant improvement in the quality of life. The term Fair Trade was unknown in his lifetime but has blossomed and expanded hugely during the first decade of the 21$^{st}$. century. Jack would be delighted.

A more fundamental example is the need to re-distribute income and wealth. A reviewer of *A Contributive Society* wrote: *'It may be regarded as a companion volume to Mr Tawney's Acquisitive Society, for while Mr Tawney is mainly occupied with the fundamental disease of our economic system, Mr Bellerby tries to point the way to a new order.'* Jack was a 'doer' as well as a thinker and his ideas were fundamentally influenced by his abiding Christian faith. When Education Services reprinted the book in 1988, Sir Austin Robinson, Professor Emeritus of Economics at Cambridge, wrote in his Foreword:

> *The thinking of the book is the complete antithesis of much currently dominant economic doctrine and the argument that the more selfish we are, the more we shall benefit the human race. It (the book) is built on the idea that one should concern oneself with the treatment of one's neighbours. That philosophy is by no means dead. Bellerby will be remembered …. for this book and its consequences.*

Austin Robinson also wrote, ' *in some curious way the institutions that Bellerby inspired have survived.'* He wanted to bring together groups of contributive people, and founded a charitable fund, Education Services, to make grants to contributive people. As an academic, he envisaged that such grants would be primarily around education, hence the name.

Jack termed his philosophy 'contributive'. His concept of a 'contributive person' was one who puts more into society than s/he takes out and his thesis was that if there was a sufficient number of contributive people, there would be a net improvement in the quality of life for everyone. Input might be in terms of time, ideas, or money. The two most significant counter-cultural projects of my life story, Daily Bread Co-operative and The Neighbours Community, both owe some of their contributive philosophy to Jack who spent years, like me, seeking practical ways to express his deeply-held Christian faith.

He was wounded in World War I and lost an arm. His wife, Rosalind, became his amanuensis and lifelong companion and, in a sense, I became the son they never had. In the 1970s Jack insisted on paying for some of my writing about employee-ownership to be published.

Jack worked at the Agricultural Economics Unit at Oxford during the latter part of his career and was a familiar figure, cycling in crowded streets despite the inconvenience of having only one arm. He could also tie his own shoelaces and successfully challenged others in time trials!

Jack died in 1977 aged 80, and therefore he never saw Daily Bread Co-operative, which Rosalind declared was the best outworking of his philosophy. She spent years collecting and editing his papers and donated a beautiful tapestry which hangs in the meeting room at Daily Bread. They were both inspirational friends to Susan and me.

# Appendix B: Letter from Rosalind Bellerby

**(Minute Book.Vol.2 1987 p.65)**
Rosalind Bellerby was the first of only two people to become Honorary Members of The Neighbours Community. She was an occasional visitor from Oxford until she moved into a residential home. Rosalind died in 1993.

36 Norham Road
Oxford
OY2 6SQ

29 November 1987

Dear Friends (Anne, Claire, Jayne, Michael, Richard, Roger & Susan)

I write with warmest greetings to you all and with many thanks for the return of the loan I made to you. It is pleasing to know that the loan bridged a gap which made it possible to achieve your purpose of including 140 Ardington Road in your Neighbours scheme.

I am honoured by your invitation to become an Honorary Member of The Neighbours and although I have little to contribute except good wishes, I am happy to accept. In these days it is difficult to get over to visit you but unexpected opportunities have a habit of turning up and in the meantime I look forward to hearing of your progress.

With best wishes for Christmas and the new year, and love to you all,

Rosalind

# *Appendix C: In Memoriam - Hercules*

**(Minute Book 1991 Vol.4 p.56)**

Hercules was a short-tempered border terrier. He was part of our household since Mary's O-level year. Early in the summer of 1991 he became ill and had to be put down on 25 June. He was 16 years old, well over 100 dog-years. Puss belongs to Edith. Sammy, a handsome ginger cat came with John and Jenny. The following scene might have taken place recently.

Hercules is in the garden, sniffing about among the roses. He is surprised to come face to face with Sammy...

Hercules:          Hello. Er, you're new here aren't you?

Sammy:             Yes, my name's Sammy.

Hercules:          I'm Hercules. For strength you know. My friends call me Herc, but you'd better stick to Hercules until we know each other better. I reckon to be in charge round here so I hope you're not going to be any trouble. Ignore that awful black Puss. Where are you from?

Sammy:             Towcester.

Hercules:          Toaster? Is that anywhere near Abington Park? That's the centre of the world, of course.

| | |
|---|---|
| Sammy: | I've never heard of Haddington Park. |
| Hercules: | Well, I've never heard of Toaster. Perhaps it's near Daily Bread where Roger works. Ha, ha. You can laugh at my jokes if you like. |
| Sammy: | I don't know what you're talking about but it doesn't sound very funny to me. |
| Hercules: | Hey, wait a bit. This is my patch and if I say laugh, then you laugh or I'll chase you up a tree like that black Puss. I can't see her and I can't hear her any more but I can smell her, so I'll just bark and hope for the best. |
| Puss (thinks): | I wish the silly old fool could see me so that I could spit at him and impress that Sammy. I could go a bundle on that cat. If only I had more fur and fewer of these embarrassing bald patches. I'll ask Edith for a double dose of the flea powder. |
| Hercules (thinks): | There seem to be two of them now to torment me and no respect for age or position or property rights. Mind you, that orange job, he's a real class cat with fur all over. Funny that he's never heard of Abington Park. All he can talk about is toast. Wait till I find that Puss. I'll 'toaster'. Ha ha. |
| Sammy: | Well, I dunno. I can't make out what's going on here. I'll go and ask John and Jenny. Maybe they can explain it all |

# *Appendix D: An* Agape

**(Based on a typical *agape* occasion at The Neighbours Community)**
The person leading the worship welcomes guests and outlines the liturgy.

*Leader*: Creator God, as we give thanks for this food, we remember those who are hungry. Your people cry out for justice. We ask for strength to put our prosperity to the service of the poor and disadvantaged.

*All*: Your world is one world and we are stewards of it.
*Reading. Matthew 26:26-28 NRSV*: While they were eating, Jesus took a loaf of bread, and after blessing it he broke it, gave it to the disciples and said, 'Take, eat, this is my body.' Then he took a cup, and after giving thanks he gave it to them, saying, 'Drink from it, all of you; for this is my blood of the new covenant, which is poured out for many for the forgiveness of sins.'

*Leader (holding the bread)*: This is the bread, not bought from a shop but lovingly made in our kitchen, full of seeds, risen with yeast. This is 'bread', a symbol of our prosperity which is not so much of our making but due to happenstance and by grace, the unmerited favour of a loving God, This is the bread which is broken as sometimes we feel broken, wounded, defeated by circumstances. This is the bread which is a symbol of our life together, committed to nourish each other. This is the bread, given for us, which Jesus tells us to eat together to remind us of his life and death on this earth. So, let us eat this bread in silence.

Each person breaks -off a piece of bread and gives it to his/her neighbour, then hands on the plate. Grace may be said.

Then food is brought in and the meal is eaten

*After the meal the leader (holding the cup)*: This is the wine which Jesus told us to share, in remembrance of him, and to be aware of our need for forgiveness. As we drink from this cup, let us forgive one another and all who seek our forgiveness.

The cup is passed round for each person to drink, in silence

*All*: The grace of our Lord Jesus Christ, the love of God and the fellowship of the Holy Spirit be with us all evermore. Amen.

# *Appendix E: Twelve marks of New Monasticism*

This is an abridged version of the Twelve Marks which express the common concerns of new monastic communities in USA, as suggested at a gathering in Durham in 2004:

1. Relocation to abandoned places such as inner-city deprived areas

2. Sharing economic resources with fellow community members and the needy among us

3. Hospitality to strangers

4. Pursuit of reconciliation of the divisions within the Church

5. Humble submission to the Church, Christ's body

6. Formation of a rule for the community

7. Nurturing the common life of the members of the community

8. Inclusion of singles, married couples and children.

9. Geographical proximity of community members who share the rule

10. Care for the environment, God's creation.

11. Peacemaking and conflict resolution within communities.

12. Commitment to a disciplined contemplative life

Differences from traditional Christian monasticism:

1. Traditional monastic vows of celibacy, poverty and obedience are not normally taken.

2. Communities do not always live in a single place, but geographic proximity is emphasized by the movement.

3. The movement includes married couples.

4. Members of the movement do not wear religious habits.

Taken from *New Monasticism – what it has to say to today's church*, Jonathan Wilson-Hartgrove (Brazos, 2008).

# *Further reading and sources of information*

*Community and Growth*. A classic book about Christian communities by Jean Vanier, founder of L'Arche. (Darton Longman & Todd 1979. Revised Edition, Paulist Press 1989)

*The Life and Death of Dietrich Bonhoeffer*. Mary Bosanquet. Comprehensive and authoritative biography of Bonhoeffer and his teaching. (Hodder and Stoughton 1968)

*Life Together*. Dietrich Bonhoeffer's teaching arising from the community life at Finkenwalde in the mid-1930's. Translated by John Doberstein. (Christian Kaiser Verlag 1954)

*A Contributive Society*. Jack Bellerby. First published in 1931 when Jack was Professor of Economics at Liverpool University. (Education Services 1931. A second and augmented edition was published by Education Services in 1988)

*The Church That Meets In Your House*. A short description of the cell groups which led to the initiation of The Neighbours Community. Roger Sawtell (Daily Bread Co-operative 1980)

*New Monasticism – what it has to say to to-day's church*. Jonathan Wilson-Hartgrove, a leader of the new monastic movement in USA and founding member of Rutba House community. Includes a brief history of monasticism and describes a contemporary counter-cultural lifestyle based on Twelve Marks of New Monasticism (see Appendix E) (Brazos Press 2008)

*The Different Drum*. The story of a long journey into community by American psychotherapist M Scott Peck. (Rider 1987)

*Seeds of the Word. Biblical reflections for small communities*. Peter Price (Darton Longman & Todd 1996)

*Basic Communities; towards an alternative society*. David Clark, Methodist minister and founding Honorary Director of National Association of Christian Communities & Networks (NACCAN). (SPCK 1977)

*Communities*. A description of twelve residential communities, nine in UK and three on mainland Europe. Jeanne Hinton (Eagle 1993)

*Directory of Christian Groups,Communities and Networks*. NACCAN published a series of these Directories. First edition 1980, Second edition 1984, Third Edition 1993, Fourth (and last) Edition 2000. They comprise a comprehensive record of residential communities and other groups over a period of 20 years.

*Christian Community*. The magazine of NACCAN. Issues 1-77. Extensive writing about communities from 1971 to 1997.

*Touching Place*. A newsletter about Christian residential communities. Published by The Neighbours Community. Issues 1-10 (2003 -2006)

*Communion Shapes Character*. An comprehensive discussion of the Lord's Supper and 'table worship' by Eleanor Kreider, a Mennonite with considerable experience of living in community, together with her husband, Alan. (Herald Press 1997).

*The Rule of Saint Benedict.* Translated by Abbot Parry OSB. The classic monastic Rule which has survived for 1500 years. Residential communities, both lay and vowed, have frequently drawn inspiration from Benedict. (Greenwing 1990).

*A Lifestyle of Sharing.* John Vincent describes the Ashram Community in Sheffield. (Ashram Press, Sheffield. 2009)

*Diggers & Dreamers.* www.diggersanddreamers.org.uk is a website listing 120 communities (2014), some Christian and some secular, in England, Scotland and Wales. Excellent information.

*High Street Monasteries.* A broad review of 'new monasticism' and proposal for contemporary monastic 'villages'. Ray Simpson (Kevin Mayhew 2009)

*Christian Communities.* Edited by John Vincent. Discusses intentional communities and includes descriptions of eleven of them, written by members. (Ashram Press, Sheffield 2011)

*The Fat Pigeon Flies.* An autobiography of the Sheldon Community, celebrating 21 years of the Society of Mary and Martha. Written by five members of the Community. (Society of Mary and Martha, Exeter 2007)

# Index